Stories That Kids Move

A Read-A-Loud and Activity Reference Guide

By: Mark A. Ricketts

Ricketts, Mark, 1973- ;
Stories That Kids Move To: A Read-A-Loud
Activity Reference Guide
Includes bibliographical references

Printed in the United States of America

Use any or all suggested activities offered at your own
risk, and at your own discretion, making sure to take into
account all necessary safety precautions. The author shall
have neither liability nor responsibility in the case of
injury to any person using or participating in any of the
games, activities, or strategies contained in this book.

To my wife Kristine and to my daughters Mackenzie and Campbell.

And to my mom and dad.

Thanks for always being there for me.

-M.R.

Table of Contents

Foreword

One day during a meeting, we were asked to include Language Arts in each of our teaching areas. I first considered how I could do this in my physical education classes without taking away movement time. After some time experimenting with various ideas, I decided to try to read a picture book to a Kindergarten class and have them act it out. They seemed to like it. Combining movement with a story had turned an ordinary and random warm-up activity into a memorable one. I had found a solution that actually enhanced my lessons, included movement, and integrated language arts.

I decided to try to find published children's books that I could use with my classes. Unable to find a resource, I started on the long process of checking out books and evaluating them to see if they would work with movement.

As I used more and more read-a-louds in my classes, I realized I might be on to something. One day I knew I was when I heard one of my students excitedly say, "Are we going to act out another book today?" Yes, yes we were.

The first year that I consistently used read-a-louds, two confused parents of one of my Kindergarteners came up to me at parent conferences. They told me that their son keeps coming home and telling them all about books that, he says, they read in P.E. class.

"We think he's confused and we were just wondering what he is talking about," they said. I shared that he was telling the truth and then explained how the students act out the stories as I read to them. His parents were both surprised and interested in hearing how they could do this at home.

I started thinking that it would be great to share my research and experiences with others who read to children. The idea for this resource was born.

Preface

It is well known that a child's ability to read by second grade is a vital skill needed for future learning. Whenever we can add something to their learning to help foster the ability we must strive to do so. At this same age, physical inactivity is a rising problem. Pairing read-a-louds with movement can work towards improving both aspects of childrens' lives.

As a P.E. teacher, we need to continue to develop warm-ups and lessons that are interesting and meaningful. These must also tie into our lesson goals. Read-a-louds that use movement can accomplish a P.E. teacher's goals and work towards developing the reading skills of our children.

Stories That Kids Move To- A Read-A-Loud and Activity Reference Guide gives you a quick and easy resource that allows you to find picture books that can turn reading into movement. Whether you are a physical education teacher, classroom teacher, or a parent, you've found another tool to incorporate movement into the life of any child. At the same time, you'll be helping to develop their reading skills. Use this book to find over 100 picture books that will allow you to move and read in a new and exciting way.

This book is set up so that you can find a book to read based on three things: (1) who is using it (2) the physical activity or general topic (i.e. jumping) or (3) the character(s) in the book (i.e. bears, dogs, frogs, etc.). Some books are listed in multiple categories.

In chapters three and four, select whom you are reading this book as (P.E. teacher, Classroom teacher, or Adult Reader). Then, see some thoughts about how to use the read-a-loud and activity as a P.E teacher, Classroom teacher, and Adult Reader. Movements can be modified for small areas. One of the most common modifications would be to do the movements in place instead of around the area. Another could be to use crumpled up paper balls inside if balls are needed. These books can be enjoyed in both large and small areas.
(*Large Area*- in the school gym, on a court, on the blacktop, on a field, backyard, or in the school cafeteria)
(*Small Area*- classroom, stage, hallway, driveway, or room in your house)
In chapter five, I have included health related stories as an additional resource.

There are two quick and easy activity/topic appendixes in the back of this book. Use these to quickly find an activity that goes with the topic you are covering or your child's, or children's, interests.

This book includes the titles of picture books that I

have found to be the best stories to get kids moving. There are activity ideas listed with each title for large areas (gyms and outside), classrooms, and rooms at home. Some of the books in my list are books that authors have written with the intent of focusing on certain movement skills. These are skills all children should develop to become confident and skillful movers. Some books were not written specifically for movement but naturally allow for it. All the stories will help children in all ways that a read-a-loud traditionally has helped as well.

Don't let my ratings stop you from trying a picture book. I can be tough when it comes to rating a book and even the books I rated a "1" can be fun to use. Remember the rating is only my opinion, you may find it more useful than I did. I would not have included it in this book if I didn't think it was one you should try. As you read some of the longer books, you can summarize parts so that you can get to the movement parts of the book.

Some of the older books cited in this book can be found as used books from online vendors and are worth the purchase. Often the same books can be found in school and/or public libraries as well.

If you want to try a new way to use picture books that will teach, entertain, and keep children active, you've found the best resource available. In *Stories That Kids Move To- A Read-A-Loud and Activity*

Reference Guide you'll find helpful, useful, and novel ideas and information to make your time reading aloud to children more interesting. This book will allow you to improve upon past teaching practices and help make the combining Language Arts and movement much easier. By buying this resource, you've committed to learning more about physically active read-a-louds. It's time to put this resource to use.

I hope you have great success implementing the stories and activities from this book. I am positive that your view on read-a-louds as a movement option will be change in a positive way. Please feel free to contact me if you have any questions or need help. I am more than willing to chat about anything to do with movement and Language Arts. Also, please let me know if you find a picture book that you think blends well with physical activity. I would love to add it to my list and use it myself.

Best,
Mark Ricketts

Acknowledgements

I would like to acknowledge:
Julie Kline, who started me on my journey of reflection concerning P.E. and Language Arts.

Dr. Christy Haller, my former principal, who encourages all her teachers to be free to try new ways of reaching students.

Jen Hemstreet, for her help with the cover photo.

And Chuck Ricketts for his original artwork.

Safety Warning- The author of this book is not responsible for any accidents or injuries from participating in the activities described in this book. Adult supervision is required.

Chapter 1- Introduction

"We keep moving forward, opening new doors, and
doing new things, because we're curious and
curiosity keeps leading us down new paths."
- *Walt Disney*

How To Use This Book

The purpose of this book is to give you new ways to use physical activities in with read-a-louds. This book gives you suggestions using over a hundred picture books. This book is designed so that you can look up a topic and find a corresponding picture book and activity quickly. While much of this book was designed with physical education teachers in mind, classroom teachers and parents can use the index made specifically for them.

Plan to request the picture books from your community or school library at least a month ahead of when you are going to use them. This will make sure you have them when you need them. If you plan to purchase any, be sure to order ahead of time. Delays in delivery are always a possibility. Classroom teachers or parents need to look at the weather if they plan to use an activity best done in a large space.

After you have read *Stories Kids Move To- A Read-A-Loud and Activity Reference Guide*, begin by selecting a couple picture books to use with your students or children. I recommend that you start with the book "We're Going On A Bear Hunt" or "Run, Turkey, Run." These sure-fire hits will get your students or children excited about using picture books in P.E. class and beyond. A good poem to read and act out is "Awful Ogre's Awful Dance" in the book "Awful Ogre's Awful Day." This can be used grades one through four and is full of words to explain and then experience. Reading the picture book before the day you will use it is also advised. This will speed up your delivery and will allow you to anticipate what acting out each part of the book will look like. It will also allow you to decide which, if any, pages you need to summarize. Then decide if you need any equipment.

On the day you will be reading your book to your class or child, be sure to demonstrate what it should look like as a student/child. Read the first page and then act it out yourself as the child/children sit and watch. Pause after a little and then read the next page. Stress to the children that they need to pause and cannot go on forever doing the same actions. Tell them if they hear your voice, they are to stop and get quiet. You may need to give them a verbal signal to finish each movement (I sometimes use a microphone in the gym).

Children sometimes try to hurry the moves so that they can be first to the end of the area or fastest around the area. Head this off by showing them what a good actor/actress looks like when pretending versus a student who hurries. You are looking for how good they can move, not how fast. Be sure to go over boundaries each time before reading a story. Your class or child should practice walking or running to the boundary and stopping. You can act out some of the stories along with the children as you read. Conversely, some stories are best to stop, put down the book, do an activity, and then pick up the book and continue. Once you look up the activity, you will see which method I recommend using.

The picture books listed under each section of this book are the same. They are just grouped differently for each type of reader. Feel free to use either index based on the topic or idea you are looking for. You can also suggest books and activities to others who read to children. Modify any suggested activities to fit your needs or available space.

Chapter 2- Using Read-A-Louds and Movement

"Reading aloud with children is known to be the single most important activity for building the knowledge and skills they will eventually require for learning to read."-Marylin Jager Adams, PhD

The Value of Read-A-Louds

After looking at over 10,000 studies, the U.S. Department of Education Commission on Reading found a clear fact. The most important thing needed for future success in reading is to read aloud to children (Anderson, Hiebert, Scott, & Wilkinson, 1985). Whether the reader is a teacher, parent, or other adult, read-a-louds give children a connection to reading. It is hard to find a reason to not read aloud to children as much as is possible. Fountas and Pinnell, experts in reading instruction, posted on their blog in January of 2019 that "Interactive read-aloud is the foundation of a community that share literary understandings through thinking and talking together." With the clear value of read-a-louds, we need to find books for read-a-louds that will interest and excite children. This will help them continue to improve both their reading ability and their reading stamina.

In school settings, students generally enjoy read-a-louds. They give the classroom a shared reading experience. "Teachers who implement interactive read-a-louds in their classrooms tend to foster comprehension, promote independent thinking, and improve thinking through discussion" (Bernardo & Dougherty, 2005). When I read a book aloud as students interact with it, students are then excited to read that book again. Read-a-louds also let students experience books and genres that they may not have chosen themselves. The exposure to different types of stories will expand their options as they choose their own books to read.

Movement and Read-A-Louds: A perfect combination

There are many proponents of interactive read-a-louds. Yet, most miss an important aspect in their description of "interactive." That missing aspect is movement. As an added bonus, using gross motor movements to act out a picture book opens up a new way to excite kids about reading. It also allows students to remember what was read to them. Mandan and Singal (2012) felt that "actions that are executed should be remembered better than those that are read about."

In his book, "Teaching With the Brain In Mind," Eric Jensen said, "Movement can be an effective cognitive strategy to (1) strengthen learning, (2) improve memory and retrieval, and (3) enhance learner motivation and morale." (Jensen, 2005) This is a win-win-win situation. As they see the illustrations between pages that I read, my students feel like they are a true part of the story. They can hear the words and then feel and see their meanings. Pica (2007), a movement specialist, agreed that when kids actually perform the words read aloud, the words become more concrete. Pica feels that when kids physically show verbs and adverbs, word comprehension increases. Acting out words such as shake, flap, quickly, and nervously allow kids to engage in authentic learning.

Moreover, young children prefer, and learn best through, active learning.

Chapter 3- P.E. Teachers Using Read-A-Louds and Movement Before or During A Lesson

"Tell me and I forget. Teach me and I remember. Involve me and I learn." –Benjamin Franklin

Picture Books in P.E.?

Forty eyes looking at me. Twenty Kindergarteners ready to move. As I open the book and begin to read, we hear about a giraffe named Gerald who can't dance. We act out his flailing moves and his sadness as he walks away. We empathize with him.

As the story moves along, we experience different animals' dances. The students love it. I show each illustration before we try the dance move. The story goes back to what Gerald is doing as a cricket tells him to listen to nature. This part I summarize because there are more words than movement. Gerald realizes that his swaying and moving is his type of dance and goes back into the animal circle to show all the other animals. He gains confidence as he dances and shows off incredible moves that leave the other animals speechless. The story ends telling everyone that he or she can dance in his or her own way. Students then take turns in small groups being Gerald, standing in front of the other animals, and coming up with their own dance move. The other students then copy the movement. We then do a sequence of sharing our moves to the tune of "Did You Ever See A Lassie?"

Before I used picture books in P.E. class, I usually did an unrelated warm-up before this dance lesson. Then I asked the students to create a move in front of others and then performed it to the song. Students struggled to have the confidence to show a move even after some examples were given. With the story, there is much more buy in from the students. They are not out there alone, Gerald is. They have learned from the story that their move does not have to be some exotic move. It can be any movement to music. The book has taken an ordinary dance lesson and made it one of my, and the students,' favorites.

I recommend using read-a-louds with picture books for three main reasons. You can use them as (1) a lead in or general warm-up, (2) as part, or all, of the lesson, and (3) a way to keep students on task and focused during a lesson.

First, picture books can be a great lead in to your lesson. For example, a quick read of Mo Willems "Watch Me Throw the Ball" before your lesson on throwing can be the hook that gets students excited to learn the correct way to throw the ball. Then they can teach Piggie (a character in the story) the proper steps. Other stories can act as a general warm-up for students. These warm-ups use imagination as a way for students to get their creativity flowing and are enjoyed by everyone. There is a high activity level when using the stories for warm-ups and some tie right into your lesson focus. Tag games are great, but having warm-ups that tie into your lesson is an even more effective use of time.

Second, picture books can be the lesson or lessons. The story itself actually enhances the lesson or lessons. While using some books like "Go, Dog, Go!" by Eastmen (2010), the teacher can pause to allow corresponding movements and then continue once he or she has everyone's attention. As you read, the students, using a hoop as a prop, act out the book.

Other books can be read in short sections with activities between the readings. In "Socco and Slurpie's Island Adventure", the main characters show a pirate different ways to travel down the plank. They are then given a chest of treasure for their trouble. They end up losing the treasure in the sand at the end of the book. I use the short sections of the book as stopping points. At each stopping point, we do a related activity (i.e. the movement the pirate learns, or using pathway treasure maps to search for the missing treasure). Students then create their own map to take home. This is a lesson I could sell tickets to enter. "Clean Your Backyard" by Lynne Hefele is another book that can be acted out as the class progresses through the parts of the book as well.

Lastly, I recommend using picture books as a way to keep students on task and keep behavior problems to a minimum during that time in your class. Younger students can be a challenge to teach for forty-minute periods. As a teacher, you need to change what they are doing multiple times. The story gives you another activity that you can use in your bag of tricks. As I stated earlier, when working on jumping in Kindergarten we read the book "Fox and the Jumping Contest" by Corey Tabor as a hook to want to get better at jumping. After reading the story, I tell them that we will have our own jumping contest at the end of the lesson, but we cannot cheat like the fox did in the story. We have to learn the right way to jump and practice like the other animals in the story. You would think they are training for the Olympics! Students are on task. What's more, they want to be learning how to jump the right way so they can do their best.

Stories can help them focus on what we are doing or bring them back to a focus. Students enjoy being part of the story and usually act accordingly.

Of course, one additional reason to use picture books and read-a-louds in physical education class is to help children learn to read. Any extra time that students can spend hearing a story will have additional benefits for the student as a whole person.

These read-a-louds in class have encouraged my students to check out the book we read, act out books at home, and even create their own book. When I set out to try to fit language arts into my classes, I never imagined I'd find a way that would enhance my lessons and not take away a moment of my limited time with the students.

If you're not using read-a-louds in Pre-School through Second grade P.E. classes, you don't know what you and your students are missing.

P.E. Teacher Stories and Activity Index
(Mark's P.E. teacher Rating Scale- **4** *(You have to use it)* **to 1** *(You could use it)*

General Warm-ups/ Creative Movement:

"A Frog In the Bog"-Wilson (2003)
-Students act out the insects in the story as the story reviews what has been eaten so far; can also act like the frog getting bigger the more that it eats.
-My rating- 3
-Best grades- Pre K-1
-Great rhyming book

"Are You Ready to Play Outside?"-Willems (2008)
-Run, skip, jump, rains, act like worms playing in rain.
-My rating- 2
-Best grades- Pre-K-1
-Elephant and Piggie book, popular with students

"Awful Ogre's Awful Day" –Prelutsky (2001) Poem "Awful Ogre Dance" pgs. 12-13.
-I read the poem once and explain the difficult words. Then students can act out dance moves as teacher pauses after the Ogre does them in the story.
-My rating-4
-Best grades-1-4
"A Winter Walk"-Barasch (1993)
-Class could pretend to go on a walk while you read or you could read then go on a walk outside.
-My rating- 1
-Best grades- Pre k-1

"Baby Bear, Baby Bear What Do You See?"-
Martin/Carle (2007, 2017)
-Different animals do different movements.
-My rating-3
-Best grades- Pre K- Kindergarten

"Be a Friend"- Yoon (2016)
-A boy lives as a mime. Pretend different
movements and get in different poses- egg,
caterpillar, chrysalis, butterfly, pose like a tree, etc.
When the boy finds a friend who pretends with him
you can pretend together.
-My rating- 3
-Best grades- Pre-k to 1

"Bear Snores On"- Wilson (2002)
- Bear is hibernating, one at a time different animals
enter his lair and start food and a party, bear wakes
up sad that he missed the party. They start the
party again. Great for acting out the story as you go
along reading it. Creative movement. Good rhyming
book.
-My rating-3
-Best grades- Pre k-2

"Berenstain Bears- Ready, Set, Go"-Berenstain
(2012)
-Class can act out while you read- running, jumping,
climbing, diving, driving, springing, swinging,
sleeping.
-My rating- 2
-Best grades- Pre k-1

"Duck and Hippo In the Rainstorm"- London (2017)
-Duck and Hippo walk through the rain and share an umbrella. Would be good for partners to do what the characters do in the story. Good story.
-My rating- 3
-Best grades- Kindergarten-1

"Eentsy Weentsy Spider"- Cole (1991)
-Follow the movements in the story.
-My rating- 2
-Best grades- Pre k-1

"Follow Me"- Sandall (2015)
-A lemur asks the reader to "follow me." Chase, race, climb, jump, hop, leap, etc.
-My rating- 2
-Best grades- Pre k-Kindergarten

"From Head to Toe"- Carle (1997)
-Have students perform the animal movements in the book. Then use the song "Animal Action" from the "Kids in Motion" CD.
-"I can do it" repeats throughout book, so you could use it before a discussion on confidence and trying new movements.
-My rating- 2
-Best grades- Pre k- Kindergarten

"Gemma and Gus"- Dunrea (2015)
-Gus follows Gemma and does everything she does. Then one day Gus goes out on his own and Gemma follows him. Good book to read while partners take

turns acting out the movements and actions that the characters do in the story.

-My rating- 3

-Best grades- pre K-1

"Go-Go-Go!"- Goldin (2000)

-Use in beginning of year when teaching waiting for the Go signal.

-Story goes through a bike race, encourages character to keep trying, great action words.

-Have students run in a clockwise circle around the gym each time you say "Go-go-go!" when reading the story.

-After the story, practice things with the "go" signal. Talk about cheering for others instead of being the negative character in the story.

-My rating- 4

-Best grades-Pre k-2

"Hanks Big Day- the story of a bug"- Kulman and Groenink (2016)

-Hank is a pill bug. He crawls, shimmies, nibbles, creeps, gets scared, climbs, curls up, scoots, crosses a street, lumbers, stops, watches a boy on a skateboard, finds his friend, pretends to fly, runs, takes a snack break, crawls, runs again, make a landing, then goes back through the motions and then falls asleep. Stresses friendship.

-My rating- 3 or 4

-Best grades- Pre K-Kindergarten

"Hooray For Fly Guy"-Arnold (2013)
-Act out as a warm-up: Kick, catch, jumping jacks, touchdown dance, secret play-pass pattern. It is a funny book.
-My rating-2
-Best grades- Pre k-1

"How to Catch the Easter Bunny"- Wallace (2017)
-Students can pretend to be the bunny who avoids many traps in different ways.
-My rating- 2
-Best grades- Pre- k to 1

"I Am (Not) Scared"- Kang (2017)
-Two friends disagree over one being scared or not. They go on a roller coaster. Goes through things students could act out. - snakes, spiders, lava, ants, aliens, whooshing on a roller coaster, at first being scared, then having fun.
-My rating- 1
-Best grades- Pre k-1

"In the Small, Small, Pond"-Fleming (1991)
-Wiggle and jiggle, waddle, wings quiver, eyes close, plunge, scatter, swirl and twirl, scoop, crab claws, dip, flip, splash, pile, pack, stack. Winter freeze, sleep.
-Act out as you read. Could have some students go into the circle (pond) and act out movements as an introduction to creative movements.
-My rating-2
-Best grades- Pre k-Kindergarten

"Jiggle, Wiggle, Prance"- Noll (1987)
-Movements to action words while standing and moving, verbs.
-Thirty-six words, and thirty-three of them action verbs.
-My rating- 2
-Best grades- Pre k-Kindergarten

"Joey the Kangaroo"- Saunders (2010)
-Kangaroo goes through neighborhood exercising.
-Act out what he does in the story.
-My rating- 3
-Best grades- Pre k-1

"Loudmouth George and the Big Race"- Carlson (2011)
-Running and Walking, training to be in shape.
-My rating- 2 (a little long)
-Best grades- Pre k-2

"Monkey Do"-Ahlberg (1998)
-Acting out what the monkeys see. Bouncy Kangaroo, climbing giraffe's neck, scram when a lady yells scram, peel and eat banana, hide under a sheet, act like traffic, pretend to play soccer, write on blackboard, climb up flagpole, swing from tree to tree, and run from crocodile at end.
-My rating- 3
-Best grades- Pre k-1

"Monkey Goes Bananas"- Bloom (2014)
-Monkey tries to get to bananas on a close island but a shark is in the way. Limited words, no sentences. Funny book.
-Act out book as you go through. Pretend to: dip toe in water, swim, run from shark, walk on stilts, fall in hole, run back from shark, use a fishing pole, chomp like a shark, escape shark's mouth, throw lasso, tug on rope that is pulling you, grab banana and hang from a tree, drop banana.
-My rating- 2
-Best grades- Pre k- 1

"My Shadow"-Stevenson 1990
-Use with creative movement. Use a light to project shadow onto a sheet, and then perform a shadow movement show at a creative movement station.
-My rating- 3
-Best grades- K-4

"Ninja!"- Chung (2014)
-A ninja sneaks, creeps, tumbles, hides and is fast... talks about some obstacles he encounters.
-My rating-2
-Best grades- Pre k-Kindergarten.

"Ninja Bunny"- Olson (2015)
-A bunny learns to be a ninja. Sneaky, strong, invisible (**unfortunately references ninja weapons** but only shows carrots, spatula, forks and main weapon of a broom as weapons. There is also a soccer ball in the illustration), able to escape, climb,

balance, fly, and show off karate moves. He learns in the end that he needs friends to help him.

-Could just skip the weapons illustration and just tell them he was holding a broom, or just not read that part.

My rating- 2 (because of the weapon reference)

Best grades- Kindergarten-2

"The Only Lonely Panda"- Lambert (2017)

-Panda looks for a friend. It dances, bounces, leaps, stomps, tail wiggle, and plays with a friend at end.

-My rating- 3

-Best grades- Pre K-Kindergarten

"Off We Go!"-Yolen (2000)

-Animal movements, tiptoe, hippity hop, dig, slither, dash, creep crawl, puts all together at end.

-I like to use for a gymnastic warm-up with 3-4 students per mat, doing movements and avoiding others.

-My rating-4

-Best grades- Pre k-1

"Pigs Can't Fly"-Cort (2002)

-The pig tries to mimic animals, trot, mimic a tall giraffe, falls down, mimic an elephant, kangaroo, bird, monkey, and finally pig rolling in mud. Students could act it out as you read.

-The pig is not satisfied at what it can do so it tries to do what other animals do for more fun.

-My rating-1

-Best grades- Pre k-Kindergarten

"Raccoons Last Race"- Bruchac (2004)
-Great story. A little long, you should summarize the end of the book after the rock rolls down the hill and the animals pass by without helping. Can have the students act out the book before that as you read. Good for going over changes of speed. Skills: Running, rolling on side, skip, jump, trot (gallop), moving slow at end of story
-A traditional folktale
-My rating- 3 (because of length, 4 if you summarize parts of the story)
-Best grades- K-2

"Shake My Sillies Out"- Raffi (1990)
-Story with action words. Can play available song afterwards to reinforce.
-My rating- 3
-Best grades- Pre k-Kindergarten

"Snowmen At Night"- Beuhner (2002)
-Read the book about what snowmen do at night. Then have exercise stations where the students do activities the snowmen do at night. Use scooters for sledding, paper plates for skating, yarnballs for snowball throw, PE equipment to build a snowman, etc.
-My rating- 2
-Best grades- Pre k-1

"Snowy Day, The"- Keats (orig. 1962)
-Good book to act out the motions of the character as he moves through and plays with snow.

-My rating- 2
-Best grades- Pre k- Kindergarten

"Spunky the Monkey"- Saunders (2010)
-An exercise adventure through the forest.
-My rating-2
-Best grades- Pre k- Kindergarten

"Stretch the T.Rex"-Saunders (2016)
-Jump, Twist, and stretch with the dinosaur.
-My rating-3
-Best grades- Pre k-Kindergarten

"Wallie Exercises"- Ettinger (2011)
-An out of shape dog sits around all day watching
T.V. A boy who owns him drives him far away and
they find a place where animals are exercising. An
elephant trainer gives the dog a workout. They go
through the terms: warm-up, hydrate, jump, hop,
spin, skip, exercise, creating own moves. Ends with
3 short activities to try- an exercise, relay, and tag
game
-My rating- 2
-Best grades- K-2

Ball Skills:

Throwing:

"Ball"- Sullivan (2013)
-A young girl plays fetch with a ball and her dog. The only word used in the story is "Ball." When the girl goes to school, the dog tries to find someone or something else to play fetch. In the end, the girl comes home and plays again.
-Could use when introducing ball skills, especially throwing.
-My rating- 3
-Best grades- Pre k-Kindergarten

"Clean Up Your Backyard"- Hefele (2014)
-Students can act out the book using yarn balls as two families try to throw trash into each other's back yards. Overhand and underhand throws are discussed. Great book.
-My rating- 4
-Best grades- K-1

"The Foot Book"-Suess (2013)
- Left and right practice- have students touch left and right foot when read in the story. This book could lead in to taking a step with the opposite foot in throwing. (Getting them to think about their foot)
-My rating-1
-Best grades – Pre-K-1

"Football with Dad"- Berrios (2015)

-Goes over all aspects of the sport football.

-Could read and then throw footballs.

-My rating-1

-Best grades- K-1

"Socco and Slurpie's Giant Problem"- Ricketts (2015)

-Overhand and underhand throw- Socco and Slurpie teach the giant how to throw overhand and underhand. Split into short chapters, you can read a chapter at a time and then work on skills. Available on Amazon.

-My rating- 3

-Best grades- K-2

"Watch Me Throw the Ball"- Willems (2009)

- Throwing- Elephant talks about practice and working hard to learn throw. Piggie just wants to have fun and ends up throwing it backwards. I read this then hand out the yarn balls and let the students throw it like Piggie for a minute or two. I then say that you don't need to be an expert to have fun throwing, but the more you practice the better you get. We then practice underhand and overhand throwing.

-My rating- 4

-Best grades- Pre k -2

Catching:

"Beverly Billingsly Can't Catch"- Stadler (2004)
- Catching, tossing practice- Start reading on the 11th page of the story "The next afternoon..." Finish on page 18 with the sentence "But it does make sense," Then flip to the third to last page for a review of the steps of a catch starting with the sentence "Keep your eyes on the ball..." (Picture of main character catching). Finish with the sentence "Gotcha! Shouted Beverly..."
-My rating- 2
-Best grades- Pre k-1

"Can I Play Too?"- Willems (2010)
-A snake wants to catch with Piggie and Elephant but has no arms. They eventually figure out how to include the snake in their catching. Good lead in to the important parts of a catch.
-My rating-3
-Best grades- Pre k-2

"Socco and Slurpie's Giant Problem- SOLVED"- Ricketts (2017) – sequel to Giant Problem
- Catching, underhand and overhand review. Socco and Slurpie cook the giant breakfast as they teach him to catch. They then finish their hike and meet a family camping. Practices catching and then the second half of the book reviews the overhand and underhand throws. Could lead into a throwing

carnival set up around the gym in stations. Available on Amazon.

-My rating- 3

-Best grades- K-2

Dribbling:

"Berenstain Bears Get Their Kicks"- Berenstain (1998)

-Kicking, dribbling, and passing with feet-Give students a quick summary of story. Then start on page 19 with sentence "Brother and Sister were right at the center..." Read those two pages showing the skills trap, dribble, pass, follow through, and foot volley. Only two pages to read.

-My rating- 1- Story is too long

-Best grades- Pre k-1

"Cereal Soccer"- Hefele (2008)

-Soccer skills of dribbling, trapping, passing, shooting. Partners can act out the story as it is read. Comes with lesson plan ideas as well. Written by a fellow P.E. teacher. Available on Amazon.

-My rating- 3

-Best grades- 1-2

"Hamburger Hockey"- Hefele (2015)

-Hockey Skills with same characters as in "Cereal Soccer."

-My rating-2

-Best grades 2-4

"Let's Play Basketball"-Smith Jr. and Widener (2004)

-Good as a warm up- **doesn't focus on dribbling,** action words: bounce, dribble, spin, dance, hold, flick, go, twist, turn, skip, rise, leap, and swish

-My rating- 2

-Best grades- Pre k-2

"Socco and Slurpie Meet the Princess"-Ricketts (2018)

-Socco and Slurpie meet a princess in the land of their ancestors. They must impress a king with their dribbling skills to escape the dungeon. Discusses three types of dribbling- hand, foot, stick and mentions juggling. Available on Amazon.

-My rating- 3

-Best grades- Pre k-2

"Swish"- Hefele (2014)

-Hand dribble, passing, pivoting, and shooting are discussed.

-My rating- 3

-Best grades- 1-3

General Ball Skills:

"H.O.R.S.E. a game of basketball and imagination"-Myers (2012)
-Two kids use their imagination to make impossible basketball shots possible.
-Could use when practicing shooting in a basketball basket or when trying to get a ball to land in a hoop.
-My rating- 1
-Best grades- Kindergarten-4

"Duck & Goose"- Hills (2006)
-Duck and Goose think a ball is an egg until the end of the story. Last pages tell what the ball does. ----
-Could use when talking about ball care or kicking.
-My rating- 1
-Best grades- Pre k-Kindergarten

"Socco and Slurpie in P.E. Class"- Ricketts (2017)
- Goes over changes in force with bouncing, kicking, rolling. Warms up with a hula-hoop.
-My rating- 2
-Best grades- Pre k-2

Kicking:

"Berenstain Bears Get Their Kicks"-Berenstain (1998)
-Kicking, dribbling, passing with feet
-Give students a quick summary of story. Then Start on page 19 with sentence "Brother and Sister were right at the center..." Read those two pages showing

the skills trap, dribble, pass, follow through, and foot volley. Only two pages worth reading.
-My rating- 1, story is too long
-Best grades- Pre k-1

Volleying:

"Bugs and Bubbles"- Hefele (2013)
- Bugs practice various volleyball skills. Good book to take students through volleying activities with trainer balls or balloons. Written by a fellow P.E. teacher. Found on Amazon.
-My rating- 4
-Best grades- 1-3

Striking/Batting:

"Bugs, Flowers, and Berries"- Hefele (2016)
-Overview of different ways to exercise as well as striking with a racket.
-My rating- 2
-Best grades- K-2

"Widget's Batting Lesson"- Hefele (2012)
- Friends try to teach younger boy how to play t-ball. Written by a fellow P.E. teacher. Found on Amazon.
-My rating- 2
-Best grades- 1-3

Dance:

"Animal Boogie, The"- Harter (2000)
Bear shaking, swinging through trees, stomping, flying-flapping wings, leap, slither, swaying. After story, there is a review of just the movements without the story as the students perform the "Animal Boogie" Dance. Song in the back of book could be learned in Music class.
-My rating- 3
-Best grades- Pre k- Kindergarten

"Awful Ogre's Awful Day" –Prelutsky (2001) Poem "Awful Ogre Dance" pgs. 12-13. (Note: listed in General Warm-up section as well)
-Students can act out dance moves as teacher pauses after Ogre does them.
-My rating-4
-Best grades-1-4

"Barnyard Dance"- Boynton (1993)
-To introduce square dance moves. Read first and show pictures with students close, then act out as you read along with students spread out.
-My rating- 4
-Best grades- K-2

"Barnyard Dance"-Martin (1986)
-About half way through the book, it describes a boy coming to dance with all the barn animals. You could use this if you summarize the first part of the

story and have the students act out the dance moves.

-My rating-1

-Best grades- Kindergarten-2

"Bearobics"- Parker (1997)

-Good book to start out dance unit and discuss listening to the beat. Act out the movements in the book with the class as you read. Swing, hopping, bopping, jumping, shoulder shimmy, fandango, hippy shake to left and right, slide, bounce, high kicks, disco, tango, jitterbug, marching, stamping.

-My rating- 3

-Best grades- Pre k-1

"Dancing Feet"- Craig (2010)

-A ladybug, elephant, duck, caterpillar, bear, lizard, and group of kids dance like the animals in the story. Read to class as you act it out.

-My rating- 2

-Best grades- Pre k- Kindergarten

"Down By the Cool of the Pool"- Mitton (2002)

-Great book where the frog asks different animals if they can dance like him. They cannot, but they each show them how they can dance. They all end up in the pond doing their dance moves. Great action words.

-My rating- 4

-Best grades- Pre k-1

"Earth Dance"- Ryder (1996)

-Book asks the reader to imagine himself or herself as big as the earth. It has great action words for students to act out. Great book.

-My rating- 4

-Best grades- Pre k-2

"Elephants Cannot Dance"- An Elephant and Piggie Book. – Willems (2009)

-Tells how everyone can dance. Students can act out a couple movements and then dance like the elephant does. Good to read to class at beginning of a creative dance or dance unit. Many pages to turn with only a couple of words on each page.

-My rating- 3

-Best grades- Pre k-2

"Giraffes Can't Dance"- Andrene (2001)

-Each animal dances to a different dance. Includes: waltz, rock and roll, tango, cha-cha, Scottish reel, violin dance. You could both play the different kinds of music and have the students dance or just have them quickly try each dance as you read. Good book to read as you start your dance unit. NEED TO SUMMARIZE THE PAGES IN THE STORY INVOLVING THE CRICKET AS THEY MAKE THE BOOK LONG. Message is that everyone can dance in his or her own way, uses creative movement. I read this story and then split into four small groups. I have each student take turns being "Gerald" (from the story). Standing in front of their group showing a movement (Can be from the story or a made up

one) that his/her group copies. Students take turns. You could then try the movements to the song "Did You Ever See A Lassie?"
-My Rating- 4
-Best grades- Pre k-1

"I Got the Rhythm"- Schofield-Morrison (2015)
-Girl does movements to the rhythm she hears.
-Could use when introducing moving to the beat.
-My Rating- 3
-Best grades- Pre k-1

"Moon Dance"- Asch (1993)
-Good before doing a dance with partners. Start by reading first part as they sit. Ask them to stand when the bear dances with the fog. Have them pretend to run outside and show some dance moves as you read. Then have them pretend to do the actions the bear does, like picking up toys, doing dishes, etc. Then have them run outside and dance with the rain. Finally, jump in the puddle and dance with the moon's reflection.
-My rating- 3
-Best grades- Pre K-Kindergarten

"Socco and Slurpie Cut A Rug"- Ricketts (2016)
-Socco and Slurpie go watch and perform kinds of dance: creative with ribbons, folk, square, and line dance at a dance competition. Can be read and used during a dance unit.
-My rating- 2
-Best grades- Pre k- 2

Fitness Focus:

"Exercise" (Looking After Me series) - Gogerly (2008)
-Gives a good overview of how to exercise to stay healthy. Students can act out the exercises and activities done in the story.
-My rating- 3
-Best grades- K-2

"I.Q. Gets Fit"- Fraser (2007)
-I.Q. goes through what it takes to be fit-eating healthy, exercise, sleep, drink lots of water, and stretching/warm-up. I.Q. improves his fitness as the story goes on. Could use when talking about fitness or right before and after exercising. A little long, but good if you read 1/2 then other half either next class or after exercise. I take them out to do a warm-up jog, stretch, and then a distance run when the mouse starts exercising in the story, then bring them back in, and finish the story.
-My rating- 4
-Best grades- Pre k-1

"Keep Running Gingerbread Man"- Smallman (2014)
Good story about getting fit. Different animals try to catch the gingerbread man but most are not fit enough. A little long.
-My rating- 3
-Best grades-Kindergarten-2

"Stretch"- Cronin (2009)
-Shows animals stretching- Students could stretch along as you read and discuss stretching.
-My rating- 2
-Best grades- Pre k-1

"Socco and Slurpie: Beginnings"- Ricketts (2017)
This pre-quell will explain how Socco and Slurpie met. Focuses on a review of ways to exercise and stay fit with a mention of healthy eating. Could use in P.E. class as an introduction to fitness. Students can act out exercises as the story is read.
-My rating- 3
-Best grades- Kindergarten-2

Force/Speed Changes

"Biggest, Strongest, Fastest"- Jenkins (1997) (Non-fiction)
-First page crawl, walk, run, hop, swim fly. Have students act out. Animals: elephant-act out biggest movements, ant-strongest for size, act out strong

movements, giraffe-act out tall giraffe, blue whale-large swimmer, shrew-sleeping in a spoon curled up, hummingbird- fast wings, Sun Jellyfish- act out dragging tentacles, spider- act out a spider crawling on hands and feet, cheetah- run your fastest, eel-swim, snail- slow motion, snake- slither, flea-jumping, tortoise- old, weak, slow

-My rating- 4

-Best grades- K-2

"Jasper and Ollie"- Willan (2019)

-Jasper the fox races Ollie the sloth to the pool. His pathway follows the dashed line. Would be good to use when discussing pathways.

-My rating- 2

-Best grades- Kindergarten-1

"Socco and Slurpie in P.E. Class"- Ricketts (2017)

-Goes over changes in force with bouncing, kicking, rolling. Warm up with a hula-hoop.

-My rating- 2

-Best grades- Pre k-1

Gymnastics:

"A, B, C"- Wegman (1994)

- Photographs of Wegman's Weimaraner dogs posing as letters.

-Good for body shapes during gymnastics. After reading, arrange students in groups of three or four.

Have groups form letters. Could take pictures to make a class or grade level book or bulletin board.
-My rating- 3
-Best grades- Pre k- 2

"D.W. Flips"- Brown (1987)
-Could read as class before teaching the forward roll to the students. Goes through the steps of a forward roll and talks about practicing and not giving up. Very Long.
-My rating- 1
-Best grades- Kindergarten-1

"Snip, Snap, What's That?"- Bergman (2005)
-Read and have students act out on mats as you read. After the story play "Alligator Tag" on mats. Teacher lays in center of eight gymnastic mats pushed together. Students crawl around quietly. Teacher (alligator) "wakes up" and crawls after students trying to tag them on foot or leg. If tagged, student yells, "Go away alligator!" (From the story).
-My rating- 4
-Best grades- Pre k-1

"Socco and Slurpie Join the Circus"- Ricketts (2014)
-Each part of the story focuses on gymnastics- beginning- rolling; next balancing, and then balances on equipment. Ends with a Socco cannon ball into a parachute. Can read throughout

gymnastic unit and then have "Circus performances" at end of unit. Available on Amazon.
-My rating-3
-Best grades- K-2

"Something Big Has Been Here"-Prelutsky (1990) (Book of poems)
-Poem called "My Snake." Read before or during the time that you have students form letters with their body and/or try making a letter with a partner. Have each of the letter snakes drawn on a piece of paper and hand a couple out to each mat holding 3-4 students. If time allows, switch letters.
-My rating- 4
-Best grades- Pre-K-Kindergarten

"Zoom, Zoom, Zoom, I'm Off to the Moon"-Yaccarino (1997)
-Read and have students pretending to take off to the moon while staying safe on gymnastic mat. Go through a story of an astronaut from when he wakes up to when he lands on the moon. Then crash lands back on earth (their mats) as students act it out safely on mats.
-My rating- 3
-Best grades- Pre k-Kindergarten

Locomotor/Traveling Movements:

Fleeing:

"Little Old Lady Who Wasn't Afraid of Anything, The"- Williams (1986)

-Pretend you are little lady on a walk. Each time an action word comes up in the story, students can act it out. Clomp, clomp with shoes, wiggle pants, shake arms, clap hands, nod hat, and flee at end. Words and actions repeat throughout story. Could use when talking about fleeing away from someone. (Also good around Halloween for a warm-up.)
-My rating-4
-Best grades- Pre k-1

General:

"Big Chickens Fly the Coop"-Helakoski (2017)

-Funny story about chickens who keep going to a new structure on the farm only to find it occupied. At each structure, there are crazy movements and then the chickens run home.
-Could do creative movements and running between places.
-My rating-4
-Best grades- Pre k-1

"Finkelhopper Frog"- Livingston (2003)

- Use before or as a review when going over hopping, jumping, or jogging. Lists hop, crawl, fly,

leap, and run at end of story. The frog hop in the story is really a jump and you can talk about the difference between jumping and hopping. Can ask students to do those movements as you say them. Also can use to talk about helping instead of making fun of someone who cannot do a movement yet.
-My rating- 2
-Best grades- Pre k-1

"Socco and Slurpie's Island Adventure"- Ricketts (2013)

-Join Socco and Slurpie as they meet a pirate who wants to learn different ways to travel the plank. They take him around the island, find, try out many locomotor skills, and end up with some treasure (Or do they?). Can have students act out as you read or read a short chapter and then do related locomotor (traveling) activities over the course of a couple days. Available on Amazon. (Unit plan available on Teachers pay Teachers)
-My rating- 3
-Best grades-Kindergarten-2

"Socco and Slurpie's Island Adventure- LOST CHAPTERS"- Ricketts (2013)

- 6 separate, short, "chapters". Each chapter is focused on two to three locomotor movements. They are written so that students can read them in small groups while they act them out. Alternately, the teacher can read them as the students act them out. These chapters fit into the timeline of the

original "Socco and Slurpie's Island Adventure" story.
-My rating- 4
-Best grades- Kindergarten-2

Hopping:

"Ready, Set, Hop!"- Murphy (1996)
-Hop or Jump to the simple Math problems in the story as the frogs try to get to places in less hops. Covers simple addition and subtraction as well.
-My rating-2
-Best grades- Kindergarten-1

Jumping:

"Fox and the Jumping Contest"- Tabor (2016)
-Fox wants to win a jumping contest and cheats with a rocket. Each animal jumps differently during the contest. Great when going over jumping.
-My rating- 4
-Best grades- Pre K-1

Leaping:

"Today I Will Fly"- Willems (2007)
-Read before teaching leaping to get them to "fly" and leap high into the air, talk about keep trying even if it seems impossible, helping others. Could use when talking about jumping high too.
-My rating- 2
-Best grades- Kindergarten-3

Running:

"Louella Mae, She's Run Away"- Alarcon (2002)
-Use when working on running and/or stopping safely. Can pause in the book after each time story says to look in a certain place for Luealla Mae. Have the students run from one end of the gym to the other and then continue the book, can work on stopping safely.
-My rating- 4
-Best grades- Pre k-1

"Oops Pounce Quick Run!: An Alphabet Caper"- Twohy (2016)
-A ball comes into mouse's hole then the dog chases the mouse until the mouse gives the ball back.
-Goes through the alphabet with each word from the story. Examples: Ball, Catch, but mostly running and chasing type movements.
-My rating- 3
-Best grades-Pre k-1

"Run Turkey Run"- Mayr (2007)
- Great book for warm-up or for when you teach about running/changing speeds. Students run for 6 seconds every time you read "Run Turkey, Run" in the book. Turkey hides with pigs in mud-roll on ground, swims in water with ducks-swim, stays with the horses- gallop, with sudden runs in between.
-My rating- 4
-Best grades- Pre k-1

Sliding:
"I Slide into the White of Winter"- Agell (1996)
-Making snow angels, sliding, pretending to sled.
-My rating- 1
-Best grades- Pre k-Kindergarten

Practice:

"If At First"- Boynton (1980)
-This is a short, good, book to read before trying a difficult skill or at the beginning of the year when talking about trying everything. Trying, Getting better are the themes.
-My rating- 1

Spatial Directions:
"Berenstain Bears and the Big Road Race"- Berenstain (1987)
-Sit students. Read book to them. Then have students stand and spread out. Have them pretend they are the fast cars, then the putt-putt car going over, under, through, and around; then yellow car hitting a pothole and flying, red flying off the cliff, blue's tires popping, green stopping at a snack bar and eating, finally act out putt-putt winning. (Could talk about gym safety).
-My rating- 2
-Best grades- Pre k-Kindergarten

"Ella May Does It Her Way!"- Jackson (2019)

-Ella May starts doing everything backwards including walking. Could use when going over changing directions.

-My rating- 1

-Best grades- Pre k-1

"Go, Dog, Go!"- Eastmen (2010)

-Good before spatial awareness activities: in, out, on, around, up, down, over, under, work, play, stop, and go. Need to summarize some parts. Read, then act out some of the pages with each student having a hula hoop (and being on it, laying under it, etc.) pick out some of the pages to do with the hoop.

-My rating- 4 (but very long)

-Best grades- Kindergarten-1

"Socco and Slurpie in the Haunted School"- Ricketts (2015)

-Describes Socco and Slurpie going through an obstacle course set up by their substitute P.E. teacher around Halloween time. Read to the class before doing an obstacle course near Halloween. Available on Amazon.

-My rating- 2

-Best grades- Pre k-2

"We're Going on a Bear Hunt"- Rosen (1989)
-Over, under, through - spatial words- act it out as you read it. Go from end to end, practice stopping on end line. Various creative movements and speed changes.
-My rating- 4
-Best grades- Kindergarten-1

"Ziny's Driving School"-Hefele (2014)
-A book about an alien in a spaceship that works on spatial directions and safety in the gym. Written by a P.E. teacher and comes with lesson and activity ideas. Book is read throughout the entire lesson.
-My rating- 3 (a little long)
-Best grades- Pre k-1

Tag/Open Space

"Rainbow Fish, The"- Pfister (1992)
-Concept of teamwork, sharing. Play Rainbow fish tag: 5-6 students are it, and tag others. If tagged, must stand and freeze. The only way to get unfrozen is for someone to underhand toss you a ball, giving you the ball to go share with someone else that is frozen.
-My rating- 2
-Best grades- 1-2

"I Love My New Toy"- Willems (2008)
-Story about throwing, then breaking a new toy. At the end, they play tag instead of throwing. Could

read before playing tag game, maybe before throwing.

-My rating- 1

-Best grades- Pre k-1

Chapter 4- Adults and Classroom teachers:
Using Read-A-Louds As An Interactive Story For Some Great Family Time, a Movement Break and/or a Lesson Focus
(It's not a brain break, it's a brain enhancer)

"You're never too old, too wacky, to wild, to pick up a book and read to a child." - Dr. Seuss

"I'm bored!"

A teacher does not want to hear those words. You've spent hours coming up with a plan for today that you made to be exciting and informative and yet you hear it, "I'm bored." If you have hit a time in your day where the class seems to be lagging, it is time for a movement break. More and more teachers are incorporating "brain breaks" or short movement activities to help students refocus. That is not a new idea. I've written this book to give you another way to get students moving, while at the same time incorporating some Language Arts. I call it a "brain enhancer."

Being a Health and P.E. teacher, I do not pretend to understand all that you do in the classroom. However, I do know that using read-a-louds and movement will give your students a new way to enjoy story time. You may even know of other ways to use the story as a springboard to what you are learning in the classroom (such as adverbs and adjectives). The possibilities are many. Please email me at maricketts@exetersd.org with any ideas so I can pass them on to teachers at my school.

As a parent or caregiver, you want the best for your child or the child in your care. When you add up all the time looking at a T.V., tablet, or computer you think, "There has to be something else that my child will enjoy that isn't on a screen." As a parent, I always looked at reading to my daughters as a time mostly before bed. Reading would calm them down, help them to one-day love books, and learn how to read. I now look at those same stories as a way to tire out your kids during the day, while at the same time getting them to love books in a different way. (Although I still believe reading with your child next to you while looking at the pages as you read is a must do activity as well). Movement to stories is another way that can get kids excited about reading. Especially for those kids who love to move but do not necessarily love reading. Check out the suggested picture books and feel free to use the ideas listed or to modify those ideas and create your own way to move to the book. I hope you and your loved one have fun exploring some great stories in a new way.

Adult Reader, Child's interest, and Classroom Stories and Activity Index

Alphabet:

"A,B,C"- Wegman (1994)
- Photographs of Wegman's Weimaraner dogs posing as letters.
- **Adult Readers**: Have the child put on black (or dark) shirt and pants. Have them use their best pose of each letter. If possible, have one or two family members join them to make the letters. Then help them create words using the cropped pictures of the letters they made on a computer. Could even print out their name using the letters they posed in. Use a light background.
- **Classroom teacher**: After reading, arrange students in groups of three or four. Have groups form letters. Could take pictures to make a class or grade level book or bulletin board.
- Best ages- 4-8
- Best grades- Pre k- 2

"Oops Pounce Quick Run!: An Alphabet Caper"- Twohy (2016)
- A ball comes into mouse's hole then the dog chases the mouse until the mouse gives the ball back.
- **Adult Reader**: -Can use this story to work on A,B,C's. Goes through the alphabet, each letter starts an action word. Can have them act it out by doing each letter's movement.
- **Classroom teacher**: Same as Adult Reader
- Best ages- 3-8
- Best grades-Pre k-1

Animals:

Alligators:

"Snip, Snap, What's That?"- Bergman (2005)

-**Adult Reader**: Read and have the child act it out on the floor/ground as you read. After reading the story play "Alligator Tag" on carpet/or grass- adult lays in center of carpet. Child crawls around quietly. Adult (alligator) "wakes up" and crawls after the child trying to tag them on foot or leg. If tagged, child yells "Go away alligator" (from the story) and continues crawling. You can also let the child be the alligator and chase after you.

-**Classroom teacher**: Read and have students act out on carpet as you read. After reading the story play "Alligator Tag" on carpet- teacher lays in center of carpet. Students crawl around quietly. Teacher (alligator) "wakes up" and crawls after students trying to tag them on foot or leg. If tagged, student yells, "Go away alligator" (from the story) and continues crawling.

-Best ages- 4-8
-Best grades- Pre k-1

Bears:

"Animal Boogie, The"- Harter (2000)

-**Adult Reader**-Bear shaking, swinging through trees, stomping, flying-flapping wings, leap, slither, swaying. After story, there is a review of just the movements without the story as the child performs the "Animal Boogie" Dance. There is a song in the back of the book you could sing together as you try the movements.

-Best ages-4-6
-**Classroom teacher**- Same as **Adult Reader**
-Best grades- Pre k- Kindergarten

"Baby Bear, Baby Bear What Do You See?"-
Martin/Carle (2007, 2017)
-Different animals do different movements.
-**Adult Reader**-Have your child do the movements done in the book.
-Best ages- 3-5
-**Classroom teacher**- same as **Adult Reader**
-Best grades-Pre K- Kindergarten

"Bearobics"- Parker (1997)
-**Adult Reader**- Act out the movements in the book with the child as you read. Swing, Hopping, bopping, jumping, shoulder shimmy, fandango, hippy shake to left and right, slide, bounce, high kicks, disco, tango, jitterbug, marching, stamping.
-Best ages- 4-7
-**Classroom teacher**-Same as **Adult Reader**
-Best grades- Pre k-1

"Bear Snores On"- Wilson (2002)
-Bear is hibernating. One at a time, different animals enter his lair and start eating food and a party. Bear wakes up sad he missed the party, and then they start the party again.

-**Adult Reader**- Great for acting out the story as you go along reading it. Creative movement. Good rhyming book.
-Best Ages-3-8
-**Classroom teacher**- Same as **Adult Reader**
-Best grades- Pre k-2

"Berenstain Bears and the Big Road Race"- Berenstain (1987) - *Best in large area
-**Adult Reader**- Read the book. Then have the child pretend they are the cars and doing the actions the characters do in the story. (See below)
-Best ages- 4-6
-**Classroom teacher**-Sit students. Read book to them. Then have students stand and spread out. Have them pretend they are the fast cars, then the putt-putt car going over, under, through, and around; then yellow car hitting a pothole and flying, red flying off the cliff, blue's tires popping, green stopping at a snack bar and eating, finally act out winning putt putt. (Could talk about safety while moving at recess).
-Best grades- Pre k-Kindergarten
-Tip- Use a hula-hoop around the child as the car or a pillow, or other object, as the steering wheel.

"Berenstain Bears Get Their Kicks"- Berenstain (1998)
-**Adult Reader**- Good story to read when discussing soccer or for soccer fans. After story, you could go outside and play a one on one game of soccer using cones or buckets as goal posts.

-Best ages-6-7
-**Classroom teacher**- Could play some mini 4 vs. 4 games of soccer using cones for goals after reading the story.
-Best grades- Pre k-1

"Berenstain Bears- Ready, Set, Go"-Berenstain (2012)
-**Adult Reader**- Child can act out while you read
-Best ages- 4-8
-**Classroom teacher**- Class can act out while you read. - Running, jumping, climbing, diving, driving, springing, swinging, sleeping.
-Best grades- Pre k-1

"Moon Dance"- Asch (1993)
-**Adult Reader**- Start by reading first part as they sit. Ask them to stand when the bear dances with the fog. Have them pretend to run outside and show some dance moves as you read. Then have them pretend to do the actions the bear does, like picking up toys, doing dishes, etc. Then have them run outside and dance with the rain. Finally jump in the puddle and dance with the moon's reflection.
-Best ages- 3-5
-**Classroom teacher**- same as Adult Reader
-Best grades- Pre K-Kindergarten

"We're Going On a Bear Hunt"- Rosen (1989)
-**Adult Reader**- Over, under, through - spatial words- act it out as you read it. Go from one end of

room or field to other end. Story has various creative movements and speed changes.
-Best ages- 5-7
-**Classroom teacher**- same as Adult Reader
-Best grades- Kindergarten-1

Chickens:

"Big Chickens Fly the Coop"-Helakoski (2017)
-**Adult Reader**- Funny story about chickens who keep going to a new structure on the farm only to find it occupied. At each structure, there are crazy movements and then the chickens run home.
-Best ages- 3-7
-Could do creative movements and running between places or running in place.
-**Classroom teacher**- same as Adult Reader
-Best grades- Pre k-1

Dogs:

"A,B,C"-Wegman (1994)
-**Adult Reader**- Have the child put on black (or dark) shirt and pants. Have them use their best pose of each letter. If possible, have one or two family members join those making letters. Then help them create words using the cropped pictures of the letters they made on a computer. You could even print out their name using the letters they posed in. Use a light background.
-Best ages- 4-8

-**Classroom teacher**- After reading, arrange students in groups of three or four. Have groups form letters. Could take pictures to make a class or grade level book or bulletin board.
-Best grades- Pre k- 2

"Ball"- Sullivan (2013)
-**Adult Reader**- A young girl plays fetch with a ball and her dog. The only word used in the story is "Ball." When the girl goes to school, the dog tries to find someone or something else to play fetch. In the end, the girl comes home and plays again.
-Could pretend to be the girl throwing and the dog fetching crumpled up paper ball with the reader.
-Best ages 3-5
-**Classroom teacher**- Pair students up and have them take turns being the girl and the dog.
-Best grades- Pre k-K

"Go, Dog, Go!"- Eastmen (2010)
-**Adult Reader**- A Dr. Seuss-like book. Have them hold a pillow or hula-hoop and act out what the different dogs do as you read and show the pages.
-Best ages-4-7
-**Classroom teacher**- Good when speaking about prepositions: in, out, on, around, up, down, over, under, work, play, stop, go; Read, then act out some of the pages with each student having a hula hoop, carpet square, or something they can hold (and being on it, laying under it, etc.). Pick out some of the pages to do with the hoop or equipment.
-Best grades- Kindergarten-1

"Wallie Exercises"- Ettinger (2011)
-**Adult Reader**- An out of shape dog sits around all day watching T.V. A boy who owns him drives him far away and they find a place where animals are exercising. An elephant trainer gives the dog a workout. Have your child go through the workout. They go through the terms: warm-up, hydrate, jump, hop, spin, skip, exercise, creating own moves.
-Best ages- 5-8
-**Classroom teacher**- Ends with three short activities to try- an exercise, relay, and tag game
-Best grades- K-2

Ducks:

"Gemma and Gus"- Dunrea (2015)
-Gus follows Gemma and does everything she does. Then one day Gus goes out on his own and Gemma follows him
-**Adult Reader**- Read each part, pausing to take turns acting out the movements and actions that the characters do in the story.
-Best ages-4-7
-**Classroom teacher**- Same as Adult Reader.
-Best grades- pre K-1

"Duck & Goose"- Hills (2006)
-Duck and Goose think a ball is an egg until the end of the story. Last pages tell what the ball does.
-**Adult Reader**- You could read it then go outside and kick or play with a ball.
-Best ages- 3-5

-**Classroom teacher**- Could read and discuss caring for equipment and then focus on playing with a ball at recess.
-Best grades- Pre k-Kindergarten

Elephants (and Piggie):

"Are You Ready to Play Outside?"-Willems (2008)
-**Adult Reader**- Act out the story. Run, skip, jump, rains, act like worms playing in rain.
-Best ages-4-7
-**Classroom teacher**- same as Adult Reader.
-Best grades- Pre-K-1
-Elephant and Piggie book, popular with kids

"Can I Play Too?"- Willems (2010)
-**Adult Reader**- A snake wants to catch with Piggie and Elephant but has no arms. They eventually figure out how to include the snake in their catching. After reading story have a catch outside or while using a paper ball inside.
-Best ages-3-7
-**Classroom teacher**-After reading the story have a short throw and catch in classroom using crumpled up paper balls or koosh type balls.
-Best grades- Pre k-2
-Elephant and Piggie book, popular with kids

"Elephants Cannot Dance"- An Elephant and Piggie Book. – Willems (2009)
-**Adult Reader**- Tells how everyone can dance. Students can act out a couple movements and then dance like the elephant does. Help child come up with three movements that they can remember and practice them. Then add music and do their dance with them.
-Best ages- 3-7
-**Classroom teacher**- make groups of four and have them come up with a four-move dance. Give class a choice of music.
-Best grades- Pre k-2

"Oops Pounce Quick Run!: An Alphabet Caper"- Twohy (2016)
-A ball comes into mouse's hole then the dog chases the mouse until the mouse gives the ball back.
-**Adult Reader**- Each letter is the next word in the story. Act out each action in the story as it is read.
-Best ages- 3-6
-**Classroom teacher**- Great story for when going over the alphabet. Many actions to act out either in place or outside.
-Best grades-Pre k-1

"Today I Will Fly"- Willems (2007)
- **Adult Reader**- You can have the child try to jump and leap high (fly) after reading the story. Also, talk about keep trying even if it seems impossible and talk about helping others.
-Best ages- 3-7

-**Classroom teacher**- Same as Adult Reader.
-Best grades- Kindergarten-3
-Elephant and Piggie book, popular with kids

"Watch Me Throw the Ball"- Willems (2009)
-**Adult Reader**- Elephant talks about practice and working hard to learn throw. Piggie just wants to have fun and ends up throwing it backwards. Read this story then hand out crumpled paper ball or koosh-type balls and let the child throw it like Piggie for a minute or two. Then say that you don't need to be an expert to have fun throwing, but the more you practice the better you get. Then have them practice underhand and overhand throwing.
-Best ages- 3-8
-**Classroom teacher**- same as Adult Reader.
-Best grades- Pre k -2
-Elephant and Piggie book, popular with kids

Fox:
"Fox and the Jumping Contest"- Tabor (2016)
-Fox wants to win a jumping contest and cheats with a rocket. Each animal jumps differently during the contest.
-**Adult Reader**- Act out the way each animal jumps as you read.
-Best ages- 4-7
-**Classroom teacher**- Act out the animal jumps as you read and then go outside and have a jumping contest for fun.
-Best grades- Pre K-1

"Jasper and Ollie"- Willan (2019)
-Jasper the fox races Ollie the sloth to the pool. His pathway follows the dashed line.
-**Adult Reader**- Read the book and then go outside and have a race to different places. In summer, have a race to a kiddie pool.
-Best ages- 5-7
-**Classroom teacher**- Have a walking partner race around the classroom with one student walking in slow motion.
-Best grades- Kindergarten-1

Frogs:

"A Frog In the Bog"-Wilson (2003)
-**Adult Reader**- Child acts out the insects in the story, as the story reviews what has been eaten so far. Students can also act like the frog getting bigger the more that it eats.
-Best ages-3-7
-**Classroom teacher**- Same as Adult Reader.
-Best grades- Pre K-1
-Great rhyming book

"Down By the Cool of the Pool"- Mitton (2002)-
Adult Reader- Great book where the frog asks different animals if they can dance like him. They cannot, but they each show them how they can dance. They all end up in the pond doing their dance moves. Act out the great action words.

-Best ages- 4-7
-**Classroom teacher**- Same as Adult Reader.
-Best grades- Pre k-1

"In the Small, Small, Pond"-Fleming (1991)
-**Adult Reader**- Have child wiggle and jiggle, waddle, wings quiver, eyes close, plunge, scatter, swirl and twirl, scoop, crab claws, dip, flip, splash, pile, pack, stack, winter- freeze, and sleep as you read.
-Best ages-3-5
-**Classroom teacher**- Could have some students go into the center (pond) and act out movements.
-Best grades- Pre k-Kindergarten

"Finkelhopper Frog"- Livingston (2003)
-Lists hop, crawl, fly, leap, and run at end of story. The frog hop in the story is really a jump and you can talk about the difference between jumping and hopping.
Adult Reader- Ask child to do those movements as you say them. Also can use to talk about helping instead of making fun of someone who cannot do a movement yet.
-Best ages- 4-7
-**Classroom teacher**- Same as Adult Reader.
-Best grades- Pre k-1

"Ready, Set, Hop!"- Murphy (1996)
-**Adult Reader**- Hop or Jump to the simple Math problems in the story as the frogs try to get to

places in less hops. Covers simple addition and subtraction as well.
-Best ages- 5-7
-**Classroom teacher**- good book to read and have the students act out outside. Useful in reviewing simple math.
-Best grades- Kindergarten-1

General (Different animals)

"Barnyard Dance"- Boynton (1993)
-**Adult Reader**- Read first and show pictures then act out each move with the child.
-Best ages-5-8
-**Classroom teacher**- Read first and show pictures with students close, then act out as you read along with students spread out.
-Best grades- K-2

"Barn Dance"-Martin (1986)
-**Adult Reader**- About half way through the book it describes a boy coming to dance with all the barn animals. You could have the child act out the dance moves from the story.
-Best ages-5-8
-**Classroom teacher**- Same as Adult Reader.
-Best grades- Kindergarten-1

"Biggest, Strongest, Fastest"- Jenkins (1997) (Non-fiction)
-**Adult Reader**- Act out the story- first page crawl, walk, run, hop, swim fly. Animals: elephant-act out biggest movements; ant-strongest for size, act out strong movements; giraffe-act out tall giraffe, blue whale-large swimmer; shrew-sleeping in a spoon curled up; hummingbird- fast wings; Sun Jellyfish-act out dragging tentacles; spider- act out a spider crawling on hands and feet; cheetah- run your fastest (in place if inside); eel- swim; snail- slow motion; snake- slither; flea-jumping; tortoise- old, weak, and slow
-Best ages- 5-8
-**Classroom teacher**- Same as Adult Reader.
-Best grades- K-2

"Dancing Feet"- Craig (2010)
-**Adult Reader**- A ladybug, elephant, duck, caterpillar, bear, lizard, and group of kids dance like the animals in the story. Read as you act it out.
-Best ages- 3-6
-**Classroom teacher**- Same as Adult Reader.
-Best grades- Pre k- Kindergarten

"Down By the Cool of the Pool"- Mitton (2002)
-Great book where the frog asks different animals if they can dance like him. They cannot, but they each show them how they can dance. They all end up in the pond doing their dance moves.
-**Adult Reader**- Act out great action words as you read.

-Best ages- 3-7
-**Classroom teacher**- Same as Adult Reader.
-Best grades- Pre k-1

"Duck & Goose"- Hills (2006)
-Duck and Goose think a ball is an egg until the end of the story. Last pages tell what the ball does.
-**Adult Reader**- You could read it then go outside and kick or play with a ball.
-Best ages- 3-5
-**Classroom teacher**- Could read and discuss caring for equipment and then focus on playing with a ball at recess.
-Best grades- Pre k-K

"Duck and Hippo In the Rainstorm"- London (2017)
-Duck and Hippo walk through the rain and share an umbrella.
-**Adult Reader**- Read then pause so that you can do the actions that the pair does in the story.
-Best ages- 5-7
-**Classroom teacher**- Would be good for partners to do what the characters do in the story. Good story.
-Best grades- Kindergarten-1

"From Head to Toe"- Carle (1997)
-**Adult Reader**- Perform the animal movements in the book. Then use the song "Animal Action" from the "Kids in Motion" CD.
-Best ages- 3-5
-**Classroom teacher**- Use as a brain break. "I can do it" repeats throughout book, so you could use it

before a discussion on confidence and trying new things as well.
-Best grades- Pre k- Kindergarten

"I Am (Not) Scared"- Kang (2017)
-Two friends disagree over one being scared or not. They go on a roller coaster.
-**Adult Reader**- Goes through things one could act out- snakes, spiders, lava, ants, aliens, whooshing on a roller coaster, at first being scared, then having fun.
-Best ages- 4-7
-**Classroom teacher**- Same as Adult Reader.
-Best grades- Pre K-1

"Off We Go!"-Yolen (2000)
-**Adult Reader**- Perform animal movements, tip toe, hippity hop, dig, slither, dash, creep crawl, puts all together at end. Repeats movement throughout book.
-Best ages- 3-7
-**Classroom teacher**- Same as Adult Reader.
-Best grades- Pre k-1

"Stretch"- Cronin (2009)
-**Adult Reader**- Shows animals stretching. Child could stretch along as you read and discuss stretching.
-Best ages- 3-7
-**Classroom teacher**- Same as Adult Reader.
-Best grades- Pre k-1

Giraffes:

"Giraffes Can't Dance"- Andrene (2001)
-Each animal dances to a different dance including: waltz, rock and roll, tango, cha-cha, Scottish reel, and violin dance.
-**Adult Reader**- You could play the different kinds of music and dance. Alternatively, just quickly try each dance without music after looking at the illustration as you read. Message is that everyone can dance in his or her own way, uses creative movement.
-Best ages-3-7
-**Classroom teacher**- Read and then split into four small groups. Have each student take turns being "Gerald" (from the story). Standing in front of their group showing a movement (Can be from the story or a made up one) that his/her group copies. Students take turns. You could then try the movements to the song "Did You Ever See A Lassie?"
-Best grades- Pre k-1

Kangaroo:

"Joey the Kangaroo"- Saunders (2010)
-Kangaroo goes through the neighborhood exercising.
-**Adult Reader**- Try the exercises the Kangaroo does.
-Best ages- 3-7
-**Classroom teacher**- Same as Adult Reader.
-Best grades- Pre k-1

Lemur:

"Follow Me"- Sandall (2015)

-A lemur asks the reader to "follow me." Chase, race, climb, jump, hop, leap, etc.

-**Adult Reader**- Act out the actions in the book.

-Best ages- 4-6

-**Classroom teacher**- Same as Adult Reader.

-Best grades- Pre k-Kindergarten

Mice:

"Cereal Soccer"- Hefele (2008)

-Mice; Soccer skills of dribbling, trapping, passing, shooting.

-**Adult Reader**- Could read outside. Stop and do what the mice are doing in the story, using a soccer ball.

-Best ages- 6-8

-**Classroom teacher**- Partners can share a ball and act out the story as you read. Comes with lesson plan ideas as well. Written by a P.E. teacher. Available on Amazon.

-Best grades- 1-2

"Hamburger Hockey"- Hefele (2015)

-Mice; Hockey Skills with same characters as in "Cereal Soccer."

-**Adult Reader**- Using hockey sticks, try the skills in the story.

-Best ages-7-10

-**Classroom teachers**- Ask the P.E. teacher when he/she is working with hockey sticks and read the day before.
-Best grades 2-4

"I.Q. Gets Fit"- Fraser (2007)
-I.Q. the mouse goes through what it takes to be fit: eating healthy, exercise, sleep, drink lots of water, and stretching/warm-up. I.Q. improves his fitness as story goes on.
-**Adult Reader**- Read half before and half after you exercise. Do a warm-up jog, stretching, and a jog/walk for 5 minutes when the mouse starts exercising in the story and then bring your child back and finish the story. Then help your child make his or her own fitness poster.
-Best ages- 4-7
-**Classroom teacher**-Read the first half of the book - up to when I.Q. starts to exercise right before recess. Encourage students to exercise at recess like I.Q. Then finish the story when they come back inside. Have each student make a fitness poster like in the story.
-Best grades- Pre k-1

"Oops Pounce Quick Run!: An Alphabet Caper"- Twohy (2016)
-A ball comes into mouse's hole then the dog chases the mouse until the mouse gives the ball back.
-Best ages- 3-8
-**Adult Reader**: Can use this story to work on A,B,C's. Goes through the alphabet, each letter

starts an action word. Can have them act it out by doing each letter's movement.

-**Classroom teacher**: Same as Adult Reader.

-Best grades-Pre k-1

Monkey:

"Monkey Do"-Ahlberg (1998)

-**Adult Reader**- Acting out what the monkey sees as you read. Bouncy Kangaroo, climbing giraffe's neck, scram when a lady yells "scram!", then peel and eat banana, hide under a sheet, act like traffic, pretend to play soccer, write on blackboard, climb up flagpole, swing from tree to tree, run from crocodile at end.

-Best ages- 3-7

-**Classroom teacher**- Same as Adult Reader.

-Best grades- Pre k-1

"Spunky the Monkey"- Saunders (2010)

-An exercise adventure through the forest

-**Adult Reader**- Do the exercises as you read the story.

-Best ages- 3-5

-**Classroom teacher**- Same as Adult Reader.

-Best grades- Pre k- Kindergarten

Monkey (and shark):

"Monkey Goes Bananas"- Bloom (2014)
-Monkey tries to get to bananas on a close island but a shark is in the way. Limited words, no sentences. Funny book.
-**Adult Reader**- Act out book as you go through. Pretend to: dip toe in water, swim, run from shark, walk on stilts, fall in hole, run back from shark, use a fishing pole, chomp like a shark, escape the shark's mouth, throw lasso, tug on rope that is pulling you, grab banana and hang from a tree, drop banana.
-Best ages- 3-7
-**Classroom teacher**- Same as Adult Reader.
-Best grades- Pre k-1

Panda:

"The Only Lonely Panda"- Lambert (2017)
-Panda looks for a friend. It dances, bounces, leaps, stomps, tail wiggle, and plays with a friend at end.
-**Adult Reader**- act out the movements in the book. Talk about what makes a good friend.
-Best ages- 4-6
-**Classroom teacher**- Same as Adult Reader.
-Best grades- Pre K-Kindergarten

Pigs:

"Louella May, She's Run Away"- Alarcon (2002)
- **Adult Reader**- You can pause in the book after each time story says to look in a certain place for

Luealla Mae. Have your child run from one end of the room or yard to the other end and then continue the book, can work on stopping safely.

-Best ages- 3-7

-**Classroom teacher**- take outside and read it on a field and have them run from one spot to another each time the characters look for Louella.

-Best grades- Pre k-1

"Pigs Can't Fly"-Cort (2002)

-The pig is not satisfied at what it can do so it tries to do what other animals do for more fun.

-**Adult Reader**- The pig tries to mimic animals, trot, tall giraffe, falls down, elephant, kangaroo, bird, monkey, and finally pig rolling in mud. Act it out as you read.

-Best ages- 3-5

-**Classroom teacher**- Same as Adult Reader.

-Best grades- Pre k-Kindergarten

Rabbit:

"Ninja Bunny"- Olson (2015)

-A bunny learns to be a ninja. Sneaky, strong, invisible, (unfortunately references ninja weapons but only shows carrots, spatula, forks and main weapon of a broom as weapons. There is also a soccer ball in the illustration) able to escape, climb, balance, fly, and show off karate moves. He learns in the end that he needs friends to help him.

-**Adult Reader**- You could just not show the weapons illustration and just tell them he was holding a broom, or just not read that part. Act out the parts of the book using a broom and carrots outside.

-Best ages- 5-8

-**Classroom teacher**- Pretend to act out book while speaking about the dangers of weapons.

-Best grades- Kindergarten-2

Raccoons:

"Raccoons Last Race"- Bruchac (2004) -A traditional folktale

-**Adult Reader**- Great story. Can have the child act out the book as you read.

-Best ages- 5-8

-**Classroom teacher**- Same as Adult Reader.

-Best grades- K-2

Sloth:

"Jasper and Ollie"- Willan (2019)

-Jasper the fox races Ollie the sloth to the pool. His pathway follows the dashed line.

-**Adult Reader**- Read the book and then go outside and have a race to different places. In summer, have a race to a kiddie pool.

-Best ages- 5-7

-**Classroom teacher**- Have a walking partner race around the classroom with one student walking in slow motion.

-Best grades- Kindergarten-1

Turkeys:

"Run Turkey Run"- Mayr (2007)
-Turkey hides with pigs in mud-roll on ground, swims in water with ducks-swim, stays with the horses- gallop with sudden runs in between.
-**Adult Reader**- Great book. Child runs for six seconds every time you read "Run Turkey, Run" in the book. If inside, have them run in place.
-Best ages- 3-7
-**Classroom teacher**- Try in your classroom or outside.
-Best grades- Pre k-1

Circus:

"Socco and Slurpie Join the Circus"- Ricketts (2014)
-Each part of the story focuses on gymnastic skills- beginning- rolling; next part balancing, then balances on equipment. Ends with a Socco cannon ball into a parachute.
-**Adult Reader**- Can read and then have "Circus performances" at end of book. Available on Amazon.
-Best ages- 5-8
-**Classroom teacher**- Ask the P.E. teacher when he/she is working on gymnastic skills and read the week or day before.
-Best grades- K-2

Dance:

"Animal Boogie, The"- Harter (2000)

Adult Reader- Act like the bear shaking, swinging through trees, stomping, flying-flapping wings, leap, slither, swaying. After story, there is a review of just the movements without the story as the students perform the "Animal Boogie" Dance. Can try singing the song in the back of the book or dancing to any music.

-Best ages- 3-5

-**Classroom teacher**- Same as Adult Reader.

-Best grades- Pre k- Kindergarten

"Awful Ogre's Awful Day" –Prelutsky (2001) Poem "Awful Ogre Dance" pgs. 12-13.

-**Adult Reader**- Act out dance moves as you pause after the Ogre does them in the story. Explain the words that are more difficult.

-Best ages- 7-10

-**Classroom teacher**- Same as Adult Reader. Look at the other poems as well.

-Best grades-1-4

"Barnyard Dance"- Boynton (1993)

-**Adult Reader**- Read first and show pictures then act out each move with the child.

-**Classroom teacher**- Read first and show pictures with students close, then act out as you read along with students spread out.

-Best ages-5-8

-Best grades- K-2

"Bearobics"- Parker (1997)
- Moves: swing, hopping, bopping, jumping, shoulder shimmy, fandango, hippy shake to left and right, slide, bounce, high kicks, disco, tango, jitterbug, marching, stamping.
-**Adult Reader**- Act out the movements in the book with your child as you read.
-Best ages- 3-7
-**Classroom teacher**- Same as Adult Reader.
-Best grades- Pre k-1

"Dancing Feet"- Craig (2010)
-**Adult Reader**- A ladybug, elephant, duck, caterpillar, bear, lizard, and group of kids dance like the animals in the story- read as you act it out.
-**Classroom teacher**- Same as Adult Reader.
-Best ages- 3-6
-Best grades- Pre k- Kindergarten

"Down By the Cool of the Pool"- Mitton (2002)
-Great book where the frog asks different animals if they can dance like him. They cannot, but they each show them how they can dance. They all end up in the pond doing their dance moves.
-**Adult Reader**- Act out great action words as you read.
-Best ages- 3-7
-**Classroom teacher**- Same as Adult Reader.
-Best grades- Pre k-1

"Earth Dance"- Ryder (1996)
-Book asks reader to imagine himself or herself as big as the earth and has great action words for kids to act out. Great book. (Poem)
-**Adult Reader**- Do the movements that the author asks you to do throughout the poem.
-Best ages- 4-7
-**Classroom teacher**- Same as Adult Reader.
-Best grades- Pre k-2

"Elephants Cannot Dance"- An Elephant and Piggie Book. – Willems (2009)
-**Adult Reader**- Tells how everyone can dance. Your child can act out a couple movements and then dance like the elephant does. Help child come up with three movements that they can remember and practice them. Then add music and do the created dance with them.
-**Classroom teacher**- Make groups of four and have them come up with a four-move dance. Give class a choice of music.
-Best ages- 3-7
-Best grades- Pre k-2

"Giraffes Can't Dance"- Andrene (2001)
-Each animal dances to a different dance including: waltz, rock and roll, tango, cha-cha, Scottish reel, violin dance.
-**Adult Reader**- You could play the different kinds of music and dance or just quickly try each dance after looking at the illustration as you read. Message is

that everyone can dance in his or her own way, uses creative movement.

-Best ages-3-7

-**Classroom teacher**- Read and then split into four small groups. Have each student take turns being "Gerald" (from the story). Standing in front of their group showing a movement (Can be from the story or a made up one) that his/her group copies. Students take turns. You could then try the movements to the song "Did You Ever See A Lassie?"

"I Got the Rhythm"- Schofield-Morrison (2015)

-Girl does movements to the rhythm she hears.

-**Adult Reader**- Read as child acts out the moves the main character does in the story.

-Best ages- 4-7

-**Classroom teacher**- Same as **Adult Reader**

-Best grades- Pre k-1

"Moon Dance"- Asch (1993)

-**Adult Reader**- Start by reading first part as they sit. Ask them to stand when the bear dances with the fog. Have them pretend to run outside and show some dance moves as you read. Then have them pretend to do the actions the bear does, like picking up toys, doing dishes, etc. Then have them run outside and dance with the rain. Finally, jump in the puddle and dance with the moon's reflection.

-Best ages- 3-5

-**Classroom teacher**- same as **Adult Reader**.

-Best grades- Pre K-Kindergarten

"Socco and Slurpie Cut A Rug"- Ricketts (2016)
-Socco and Slurpie go watch and perform kinds of dance: creative with ribbons, folk, square, and line dance at a dance competition.
Adult Reader- After each short "chapter" have them act out the dances in that chapter. After the book is over, have them do a ribbon dance if available.
-Best ages- 4-8
-**Classroom teacher**- Find out when the P.E. teacher is doing a dance unit and read the week before.
-Best grades- Pre k- 2

Dinosaurs:

"Stretch the T.Rex"-Saunders (2016)
-**Adult Reader**- Jump, twist, and stretch with the dinosaur.
-Best ages- 3-5
-**Classroom teacher**- same as Adult Reader.
-Best grades- Pre k-Kindergarten

Earth:

"Earth Dance"- Ryder (1996)
-Book asks reader to imagine himself or herself as big as the earth and has great action words for kids to act out. Great book. (Poem)
-**Adult Reader**- Do the movements that the author asks you to do throughout the poem.
-Best ages- 4-7
-**Classroom teacher**- Same as Adult Reader.
-Best grades- Pre k-2

Exercise:

"Exercise" (Looking After Me series)- Gogerly (2008)
-Gives a good overview of how to exercise to stay healthy.
-**Adult Reader**- Kids can act out the exercises and activities that are done in the story.
-Best ages- 5-8
-**Classroom teacher**- Same as Adult Reader. Read before recess.
-Best grades- K-2

"Keep Running Gingerbread Man"- Smallman (2014)
-Good story about getting fit. Different animals try to catch the gingerbread man but most aren't fit enough.
-**Adult Reader**- Read and then go for a run

-Best ages 5-9
-**Classroom teacher**- Same as Adult Reader.
-Best grades-Kindergarten-2

"Socco and Slurpie: Beginnings"- **Ricketts (2017)**
-This pre-quell explains how Socco and Slurpie met.
Focuses on a review of ways to exercise and stay fit
with a mention of healthy eating.
Adult Reader- Kids can act out exercises as you read
the story.
-Best ages- 5-8
-**Classroom teacher**- Use as a health lesson; or to
reinforce what the P.E. or Health teacher is doing.
-Best grades- Kindergarten-2

Friends:

"Be a Friend"- **Yoon (2016)**
-A boy lives as a mime. Pretend different
movements and gets in different poses- egg,
caterpillar, chrysalis, butterfly, pose like a tree, etc.
Then the boy finds a friend who pretends with him.
-**Adult Reader**- Show the illustrations and then try
each one pretending to be a mime as you read.
-Best ages- 4-7
-**Classroom teacher**- Same as Adult Reader.
-Best grades- Pre-k - 1

"I Love My New Toy"- Willems (2008)
-Story about throwing, then breaking a new toy. At the end, they play tag instead of throwing.
–Adult Reader- Could read before playing tag game outside, maybe before throwing a ball back and forth.
-Best ages- 4-7
-Classroom teacher- Could read before taking class outside on the field and playing a game of tag. Remember to demonstrate a soft tag.
-Best grades- Pre k-1

Folktales:

"Raccoons Last Race"- Bruchac (2004)
-Great story. A little long.
-Adult Reader- Act out the movements in the story.
-Best ages: 5-9
-Classroom teacher: Good story to read when discussing the meaning of a story. Have class spread out and act out between times that you read.
-Best grades- Kindergarten- 3

General:

"Ella May Does It Her Way!"- Jackson (2019)
-Ella May starts doing everything backwards including walking.

-**Adult Reader**- Read and then ask child to do different things, including walking, backwards. Join in when possible.

-Best ages- 4-7

-**Classroom teacher**- Could use when going over changing directions. Have students act out doing several classroom tasks backwards after reading story.

-Best grades- Pre k-1

"The Foot Book"-Suess (2013)

- **Adult Reader**- Left and right practice- have child touch left and right foot when read in the story. Also could lead in to taking a step with the opposite foot in throwing. (Getting them to think about their stepping foot.)

-Best ages- 4-7

-**Classroom teacher**- Same as Adult Reader.

-Best grades – Pre-K-1

"Go-Go-Go!"- Goldin (2000)

-Story goes through a bike race, encourages character to keep trying, great action words.

-**Adult Reader**- Have your child run around a yard or driveway (if available- if not have them jog slow around the room) when you say "Go-go-go!"

-Best ages- 4-8

-**Classroom teacher**s- Have students run in a clockwise circle around you in the field each time you say "Go-go-go!" when reading the story.

-After the story, practice things with the "go" signal.
-Talk about cheering for others instead of being the negative character in the story.
-Best grades-Pre k-2

"Hooray For Fly Guy"-Arnold (2013)
-**Adult Reader**- Act out: kick, catch, jumping jacks, touchdown dance, secret play-pass pattern. It is a funny book. Help plan a secret play-pass pattern and then try it out. Play some football outside if possible after reading.
-**Classroom teacher**- Ask pairs of students to come up with their own secret play or pass pattern. Have each pair show the class outside.
Best grades- Pre k-1

"Jiggle, Wiggle, Prance"- Noll (1987)
-**Adult Reader**- Do movements to action words while standing and moving to the verbs.
-Thirty-six words, and thirty-three of them action verbs.
-Best ages- 3-5
-**Classroom teacher**- Same as **Adult Reader**.
-Best grades- Pre k-Kindergarten

"Let's Play Basketball"-Smith Jr. and Widener (2004)
- Doesn't focus on dribbling.
-**Adult Reader**- Act out action words: bounce, dribble, spin, dance, hold, flick, go, twist, turn, skip, rise, leap, and swish. You could use a ball outside to help, or just have your child pretend.

-Best ages- 4-8
-**Classroom teacher**- Try reading and acting it out outside on a basketball court.
-Best grades- Pre K-2

"Loudmouth George and the Big Race"- Carlson (2004)
-Running and walking, training to be in shape.
-**Adult Reader**- Do the actions the character does in the book.
-Best ages- 4-7
-**Classroom teacher**- Read and then take a walk around the building.
-Best grades- Pre k-1

"My Shadow"-Stevenson 1990
- **Adult Reader**- Use with creative movement. Use a light projecting shadow onto sheet that hangs from shower curtain or door. Take turns standing behind the sheet making different poses and movements.
-Best ages- 4-10
-**Classroom teacher**- Perform shadow movement show at a creative movement station.
-Best grades- K-4

"Shake My Sillies Out"- Raffi (1990)
-**Adult Reader**- Act out story with action words. Can play available song afterwards to reinforce.
-Best ages- 3-5
-**Classroom teacher**- Great to do as a "brain break."
-Best grades- Pre k-Kindergarten

Halloween:

"Little Old Lady Who Wasn't Afraid of Anything, The"- Williams (1986)
-**Adult Reader**- Pretend you are little lady on a walk. Each time an action word comes up in the story, you can act it out. Clomp, clomp with shoes, wiggle pants, shake arms, clap hands, nod hat, and flee at end. Words and actions repeat throughout story.
-Best ages- 4-7
-**Classroom teacher**- Do as class as you read outside on the blacktop or field.
-Best grades- Pre k-1

"Socco and Slurpie in the Haunted House"- Ricketts (2015)
-Describes Socco and Slurpie going through an obstacle course set up by their substitute P.E. teacher around Halloween time.
-**Adult Reader**- Read before doing an obstacle course. Either set one up outside using any available equipment (such as buckets, sticks, etc.) or do a walking one inside- side roll over bed, crawl under table, walk around chairs, etc. Available on Amazon.
-Best ages- 4-9
-**Classroom teacher**- After you read it, create an obstacle course in your classroom or outside using recess equipment or borrowed equipment from your P.E. teacher. You could also let students plan and create their own mini-obstacle course or a pretend obstacle course written and drawn on

paper. Lastly, check with your P.E. teacher to see if he/she is doing an obstacle course in class and read a week before.
-Best grades- Pre k-2

Insects:

"Bugs and Bubbles"- Hefele (2013)
-Bugs practice various volleyball skills. Written by a P.E. teacher. Found on Amazon.
-**Adult Reader**- Blow up a balloon and pause to act out the moves in the story using the balloons.
-Best ages- 6-9
-**Classroom teacher**- Pair students and give each pair one blown up balloon. Read the story and you will collect balloons as the bubbles pop and as you read, you can combine groups if you would like. Works best in a larger room, gym, cafeteria, etc. Only try outside on a day with no wind.
-Best grades- 1-3

"Bugs, Flowers, and Berries"
-Overview of different ways to exercise as well as striking with a racket.
-**Adult Reader**
-Pause and try out the exercises and go outside and try to hit a foam ball with a racket or paddle if available.
-Best ages- 6-9
-**Classroom teacher**

-Try exercises as a class. You could also read before the P.E. teacher goes over striking.
-My rating- 2
-Best grades- K-2

"Dancing Feet"- Craig (2010)
-A ladybug, Elephant, Duck, Caterpillar, bear, lizard, and group of kids dance like the animals in the story
-**Adult Reader**- Have your child act like the animals as you read.
-Best ages- 3-6
-**Classroom teacher**- Read to class as you all act it out.
-Best grades- Pre k- Kindergarten

"Eentsy Weentsy Spider"- Cole (1991)
-**Adult Reader**- Follow the movements in the story.
-Best ages- 4-7
-**Classroom teacher**- Same as Adult Reader.
-Best grades- Pre k-1

"Hanks Big Day- the story of a bug"- Kulman and Groenink (2016)
-Hank is a pill bug. He crawls, shimmies, nibbles, creeps, gets scared, climbs, curls up, scoots, crosses a street, lumbers, stops, watches a boy on a skateboard, finds his friend, pretends to fly, runs, takes a snack break, crawls, runs again, make a landing, then goes back through the motions and then falls asleep. Stresses friendship.

-**Adult Reader**- Act out the things Hank does in the story as he does them.
-Best ages- 4-6
-**Classroom teacher**- Same as Adult Reader.
-Best grades- Pre K-Kindergarten

Make Believe:

Easter Bunny:

"How to Catch the Easter Bunny"- Wallace (2017)
-**Adult Reader**-Pretend to be the bunny who avoids many traps in different ways. After reading story, plan and set up a "trap" using available equipment. Try out the trap safely.
-Best ages- 4-9
-**Classroom teacher**- After pretending to do the bunny actions in the story, have partners design traps. Have concepts drawn out on paper and explained. Have the class vote on the best trap.
-Best grades- Pre- k to 2

Giants:

"Socco and Slurpie's Giant Problem"- Ricketts (2015)
-Socco and Slurpie teach the giant how to throw overhand and underhand.
Adult Reader- Split into short chapters. You can read a chapter at a time and then work on skills

outside or inside with a paper ball. Available on Amazon.

-Best ages- 5-8

Classroom teacher- Read before you PE teacher works on throwing.

-Best grades- K-2

"Socco and Slurpie's Giant Problem- SOLVED"- Ricketts (2017) – sequel to Giant Problem

-Socco and Slurpie cook the giant breakfast as they teach him to catch. They then finish their hike and meet a family camping. Practices catching and then the second half reviews the overhand and underhand throws.

-**Adult Reader**- Could lead into a throwing target carnival set up around the backyard, driveway, or even inside. Stations such as a bucket for underhand, a bucket upside down for a target, or even a tiny hole in the mulch to try to get it in. Available on Amazon.

-Best ages- 5-8

-**Classroom teacher**- Read after the PE teacher practices throwing. Then go outside and to a set-up of various throwing stations with targets on the playground.

-Best grades- Kindergarten-2

Princesses:

"Socco and Slurpie Meet the Princess"-Ricketts (2018)
- Socco and Slurpie meet a princess in the land of their ancestors and must impress a king with their dribbling skills to escape the dungeon. Discusses three types of dribbling- hand, foot, stick and mentions juggling. Available on Amazon.
-**Adult Reader**- Stop after each action in book and try to dribble. Works best outside.
-Best ages- 5-8
-**Classroom teacher**- Read before your P.E. teacher goes over dribbling.
-Best grades- Pre k-2

Karate (Ninja):

"Ninja!"- Chung (2014)
-A ninja sneaks, creeps, tumbles, hides and is fast... talks about some obstacles he encounters.
-**Adult Reader**- Act out the actions in the story as you read.
-Best ages- 4-6
-**Classroom teacher**- Same as Adult Reader.
-Best grades- Pre k-Kindergarten.

"Ninja Red Riding Hood"- Schwartz (2014)
-The wolf and Red Riding Hood battle using karate moves.

-**Adult Reader**- Could act out the moves in the story
-Best ages- 6-8
-**Classroom teacher**- Same as Adult Reader.
-Best grades- 1-3

Moon:

"Moon Dance"- Asch (1993)
-**Adult Reader**- Start by reading first part as they sit. Ask them to stand when the bear dances with the fog. Have them pretend to run outside and show some dance moves as you read. Then have them pretend to do the actions the bear does, like picking up toys, doing dishes, etc. Then have them run outside and dance with the rain. Finally, jump in the puddle and dance with the moon's reflection.
-Best ages-3-5
-**Classroom teacher**- Same as Adult Reader.
-Best grades- Pre k-Kindergarten

"Zoom, Zoom, Zoom, I'm Off to the Moon"- Yaccarino (1997)
-**Adult Reader**- Go through a story of an astronaut from when he wakes up to when he lands on the moon, then crash lands back on earth (something soft).
-Best ages- 3-5
-**Classroom teacher**- Same as Adult Reader.
-Best grades- Pre k-Kindergarten

Outside Play:

"Clean Up Your Backyard"- Hefele (2014)
-**Adult Reader**- Can act out the book using soft, or paper, balls as two families try to throw trash into each other's back yards. If inside, set up a "fence" to divide the room and use 20-30 crumpled up paper balls. Overhand and underhand throws are discussed. Great book.
-Best ages- 5-7
-**Classroom teacher**- Divide classroom with desks and use crumpled paper from your recycle bin. Have each half of the class act out the story as one of the families.
-Best grades- K-1

Perseverance

"Abracadabra! The Magic of Trying"- Giraldo (2017)
-Story about believing in yourself and never giving up. Also shows encouragement of others. Good story to read when trying something new.
-**Adult Reader**- Could read and then try a new physical skill like jump rope, hula-hoop, or throwing to a target.
-Best ages- 5-8
-**Classroom teacher**- Read and then try physical skill at recess.

-Best grades- K-2

"If At First"- Boynton (1980)
-Short, good book to read before trying a difficult physical skill. Focuses on: Trying, Getting better.
-**Adult Reader**- Read and then try a physical skill outside that your child has difficulty with (i.e. jumping rope, hula-hoop, or dribbling a basketball).
-Best ages- 4-7
-**Classroom teacher**- Same as Adult Reader.
-Best grades- pre K-Kindergarten

"Today I Will Fly"- Willems (2007)
-**Adult Reader**- Read before practicing leaping to get them to "fly" and leap high into the air. Talk about keep trying even if it seems impossible, and helping others. After reading, take them outside to try to run and leap as high and far as they can. You can mark their leap distance with chalk. Could try jumping too.
-Best ages- 5-8
-**Classroom teacher**- Have a "flying" contest outside on the playground where groups of students try to leap as far as possible. They can mark their leap distance with chalk.
-Best grades- Kindergarten-3

Physical Skills:

"Beverly Billingsly Can't Catch"- Stadler (2004)
- Focuses on: Catching, tossing
-**Adult Reader**- Read, then toss and catch with your child. You can use crumpled up paper with tape wrapped around it if you need to.
-Best ages- 4-7
-**Classroom teacher**- Same as Adult Reader.
-Best grades- Pre k-1

"Socco and Slurpie in P.E. Class"- Ricketts (2017)
-Goes over changes in force with bouncing, kicking, rolling. Warms up with a hula-hoop.
-**Adult Reader**- You can act out the moves in the story after each very short "chapter." Need a hula-hoop and a ball, or you can have them pretend.
-Best ages- 4-8
-**Classroom teacher**- Partners can act out the skills from the story outside. Each pair needs a ball.
-Best grades- Pre k-2

"Swish"- Hefele (2014)
-Hand dribble, passing, pivoting, and shooting are discussed in this book.
-**Adult Reader**- Read the story and then try out the moves using a ball with your child.
-Best ages- 6-9
-**Classroom teacher**- Read before your P.E. teacher uses basketballs in P.E. class.
-Best grades- 1-3

"Widget's Batting Lesson"- Hefele (2012)
- Friends try to teach younger boy how to play t-ball. Found on Amazon.
-**Adult Reader**- Need a batting tee, whiffle ball, and bat. Read story and then try the skills outside.
-Best ages- 7-9
-**Classroom teacher**- Read before your P.E. teacher uses tees in P.E. class.
-Best grades- 1-3

Pirates:

"Socco and Slurpie's Island Adventure"- Ricketts (2013)

- Join Socco and Slurpie as they meet a pirate who wants to learn different ways to travel the plank. They take him around the island and find and try out many locomotor skills and end up with some treasure (or do they?).

-**Adult Reader**- Can have child act out as you read or read a short chapter and then do related locomotor (traveling) activities. Good book. Available on Amazon.

-Best ages-5-9

-**Classroom teacher**s- Same as Adult Reader.

-Best grades-Kindergarten-2

"Socco and Slurpie's Island Adventure- LOST CHAPTERS"- Ricketts (2013)

-Six separate, short "chapters" are each focused on two to three locomotor movements.

-**Adult Reader**- You can read them and your child can act them out as you read, or you can have your child read and then act the movements out.

-Best ages- 4-9

-**Classroom teacher**s- This book is written so that students can read them in small groups while they act them out. Alternately, the teacher can read them as the students act them out. These are written as chapters that happened during the

original "Socco and Slurpie's Island Adventure"
story.
-Best grades- Kindergarten-2

Poems:

"Awful Ogre's Awful Day" –Prelutsky (2001) Poem
"Awful Ogre Dance" pgs. 12-13.
-**Adult Reader**- Read the poem once and explain the
difficult words. Then your child can act out dance
moves as you pause after the Ogre does them in the
story. Some of the other poems in the book are
good too.
-Best ages- 7-10
-**Classroom teacher**- Same as Adult Reader.
-Best grades-1-4

"Earth Dance"- Ryder (1996)
-**Adult Reader**- Book asks reader to imagine himself
or herself as big as the earth and has great action
words for children to act out. Great book.
-Best ages- 4-8
-**Classroom teacher**- Would be good to read on
"Earth Day."
-Best grades- Pre k-2

"Something Big Has Been Here"-Prelutsky (1990)
(Book of poems)
-Poem called "My Snake."
-**Adult Reader**- Read and have your child form

letters with the body, and/or try making a letter with you that the snake makes in the poem. You could have each of the letter snakes drawn on a piece of paper for them to look at while trying.

-Best ages- 4-5

-**Classroom teacher**- Could read when practicing the alphabet and split your students into partners to try to form the letter. Take pictures of the best of each and hang near your alphabet.

-Best grades- Pre-K-Kindergarten

Sharing:

"Rainbow Fish, The"- Pfister (1992)

-Concept of teamwork, sharing.

-**Adult Reader**- See **Classroom teacher**. Need to read to a group of 6-12 kids.

-Best ages- 6-8

-**Classroom teacher**- After reading go outside in the grass and play Rainbow Fish tag: 5-6 students are it, and softly tag others. Give a couple students a ball. If tagged, must stand and freeze. The only way to get unfrozen is for someone to toss you a ball underhand, letting you have the ball to go share with someone else that is frozen. If you have a ball and are tagged, drop it and hope that someone picks it up to toss to you.

-Best grades- 1-2

Snow:

"A Winter Walk"-Barasch (1993)
-**Adult Reader**- Could pretend to go on a walk while you read or you could read then go on a walk outside.
-Best ages- 3-6
-**Classroom teacher**- Same as Adult Reader.
-Best grades- Pre k-1

"I Slide Into the White of Winter"- Agell (1996)
-Focuses on: Making snow angels, sliding, pretending to sled.
-**Adult Reader**- Child can make pretend, or real, snow angels and sled (or pretend to sled) after you read this.
-Best ages- 4-5
-**Classroom teacher**- Same as Adult Reader.
-Best grades- Pre k-Kindergarten

"Snowy Day, The"- Keats (orig. 1962)
-**Adult Reader**- Good book to act out the motions of the character as he moves through and plays with snow.
-Best ages- 4-6
-**Classroom teacher**- Same as Adult Reader.
-Best grades- Pre k- Kindergarten

"Snowmen At Night"- Beuhner (2002)
-**Adult Reader**- Have child try to act out some of the actions in the story. See Classroom teacher below to get some ideas.

-Best ages- 4-8
-**Classroom teacher**- Read the book about what snowmen do at night. Then have exercise stations where the students do activities the snowmen do at night. Use scooters (borrow from P.E. teacher) for sledding, paper plates for skating, yarn balls for snowball throw, PE equipment to build a snowman, etc.
-Best grades- Pre k-1

Sports:

"Football with Dad"- Berrios (2015)
-Goes over all aspects of the sport football.
-**Adult Reader**- Could read and then go outside and do the things in the book. Good for children with an interest in football.
-Best ages-5-7
-**Classroom teacher**- Not recommended.
-Best grades- K-1

"H.O.R.S.E. a game of basketball and imagination"- Myers (2012)
-Two kids use their imagination to make impossible basketball shots possible.
-**Adult Reader**- Read and then go to a basketball court and play a game of H.O.R.S.E. Use a lighter, smaller, ball for younger children.
-Best ages- 5-10

-**Classroom teacher**- Split into groups of 4-5 and then go out to basketball court and have groups play a game of H.O.R.S.E.
-Best grades- K-4

Staying Safe (self space)

"Ziny's Driving School"-Hefele (2014)
-A book about an alien in a spaceship that works on spatial directions and safety in the gym. Comes with lesson and activity ideas. Story is a little long.
-**Adult Reader**- Have your child act out using a hoop as a spaceship.
-Best ages- 4-7
-**Classroom teacher**- Read in beginning of year before your P.E. teacher practices staying in a self-space. Alternatively, try with your class outside after reading and talking about self-space on the playground.
-Best grades- Pre k-1

Chapter 5- Non-movement Health Related Books For Parents/Guardians, Health, and Classroom teachers

"Reading is to the mind what exercise is to the body"

–Joseph Addison

**"Busy Body Book: A Kids Guide to Fitness"-
Rockwell (2004)**
-Jump, sprint, twist, and twirl.
-Lizzy Rockwell explains how your bones and
muscles, heart and lungs, nerves and brain all work
together to keep you on the go. Kids walk, skate,
and tumble. Could use when talking about body
systems.
Best ages-4-6

"Exercise- (Looking After Me)"- Gogerly (2008)
-Book about a boy exercising.
-Best ages- 5-7

"Give Us A Smile Cinderella"- Smallman (2014)
-Stepsisters are grumpy because of the toothaches
they get from not taking care of their teeth.
Cinderella brushes all the time and wins the prince
with her teeth in the end. A little long. Same story
as the traditional Cinderella but focuses on brushing
teeth.
-Best ages- 4-7

"Gulps, The"- Wells (2007)
-Value of exercising and eating right. Could
summarize the book as you show the students the
pictures. Talks about eating right. Exercise is
mentioned as well. A family's camper breaks down
because they weigh too much. A farmer lets them
stay on the farm where they end up liking eating
healthy and exercising: doing all the chores. Longer

book. Book could be viewed as negative because the characters are overweight in the beginning.
-Best ages-K-3

"Helping Hands Book: Zach Gets Some Exercise"- Duchess of York (2011)
-About a boy who just watches T.V. and plays video games. He does not do well in P.E. (They use the word gym). Then a new boy moves in and eventually Zach realizes that it is fun to exercise with his new friend.
-Best ages- 4-7

"Let's Be Fit"- Hallnan (2007)
-Urges readers to exercise more, eat well, and rest more. Board book. Rhyming.
-Best ages- 4-6

"Oh the Things You Can Do That Are Good For You"- Rabe (2001)
-Good overview of how to stay healthy with mentions of exercise, sneezing, healthy eating, brushing teeth, etc. Good rhymes from the Cat in the Hat.
-Best ages- 4-7

"Please Play Safe"- Cuyler (2006)
-Playground Safety.
-Best ages- 4-7

**"Rapunzel, Rapunzel, Please Wash Your Hair"-
Smallman (2015)**
-Three princes try to save her but her hair is too
oily. Story about washing your hair. A little long.
-Best ages- 4-7

**"Rodeo Ron and His Milkshake Cows"- Clifford
(2005) (Out of Print but on Amazon)**
-Tooth Care, Drinking Milk, Skipping Soda
-Really good story about drinking milk instead of
Soda. Discussion on Soda and "Sometimes" foods
(foods we should only eat sometimes). A little
action with the cows shaking. Could use for a warm-
up if you summarize beginning and start at the part
where the "Shake off" starts. Have the students
acting out the shaking part, standing, as you read
through. Would be good for lesson on teeth and
drinking milk instead of soda.
-Best ages- 4-7

Physical Educator's Quick Activity Find

General warm-up: 37-46
Ball Skills:
        Throwing: 47-48
        Catching: 49-50
        Dribbling: 50-51
        General Ball Skills: 52
        Kicking: 52-53
        Volleying: 53
        Striking/Batting: 53
Dance: 54-57
Fitness Focus: 58-59
Force/Speed Changes: 59-60
Gymnastics: 60-62
Locomotor/Traveling Movements:
        Fleeing: 63
        General: 63-65
        Hopping: 65
        Jumping: 65
        Leaping: 65
        Running: 66
        Sliding: 67
Practice: 67
Spatial Directions: 67-69
Tag/Open Space: 69-70

General Topic Quick Find

About the author

Mark Ricketts is a Kindergarten through Fourth Grade Health and Physical Education teacher at Lorane Elementary School in Reading, PA. He has been teaching there since the fall of 1997.

Mark has a B.S. in Health and Physical Education from West Chester University (PA) and a Master's degree in Elementary Education from Kutztown University (PA).

Mark enjoys teaching this age group and loves the excitement that comes along with moving and learning. He hangs out with his wife-Kristine, daughters-Mackenzie and Campbell, and two coon hounds-Hero and Hope.

Mark was hooked on children's stories while reading to his daughters before bed when they were younger. Mark has written, and self-published, 13 children's books. Twelve of his books are about "Socco and Slurpie", two living gym socks, who go on adventures that involve some kind of movement or health skill. His children's books are also sold on Amazon.com.

You can find him on Facebook @soccoandslurpie .
Visit his author page at http://bit.ly/MarkRicketts
Contact him through Facebook or at
mkricketts@ptd.net

Works Cited

Agell, Charlotte. *I Slide into the White of Winter*. Tilbury

House, 1994.

Ahlberg, Allan, and Andre Amstutz. *Monkey Do!* Walker

Books, 1999.

Andreae, Giles, et al. *Giraffes Can't Dance*. Findaway World,

LLC, 2019.

Anderson, R.C., et al. "Becoming a Nation of Readers: The

Report of the Commission On Reading."

Washington, DC: National Institute of Education,

1985.

Arnold, Tedd. *Hooray for Fly Guy!* Scholastic, 2008.

Aruego, Jose, et al. *Raccoon's Last Race: a Traditional*

Abenaki Story. Dial Books for Young Readers, 2004.

Asch, Frank. *Moondance*. Aladdin, 2014.

Barasch, Lynne. *A Winter Walk*. Ticknor & Fields, 1993.

Beaumont, Karen, and Rosanne Litzinger. *Louella Mae, She's Run Away!* Holt, 1996.

Berenstain, Stan. *The Berenstain Bears and the Big Road Race.* Random House Canada Ltd., 2003.

Berenstain, Stan. *The Berenstain Bears Get Their Kicks.* Random House Canada Ltd., 2003.

Berenstain, Stan. *The Berenstain Bears Ready, Get Set, Go!* Random House Canada Ltd., 2003.

Bergman, Mara, and Nick Maland. *Snip Snap!: What's That?* Greenwillow Books, 2005.

Bernardo, P.J., & Dougherty, D.L. (2005). "Teaching Readers to Think." *ASCD.ORG, www.ascd.org/ascd-express/vol1/102-bernardo.aspx.*

Berrios, Frank, and Brian Biggs. *Football with Dad.* Golden Book, 2015.

Bloom, C. P., and Peter Raymundo. *The Monkey Goes Bananas.* Abrams Books for Young Readers, 2014.

Bolam, Emily, and Victoria Parker. *Bearobics*. Penguin

Group, 1999.

Boynton, S. *If at First ...* Little, Brown and Company, 1980.

Boynton, Sandra. *Barnyard Dance!* Seedlings, 2017.

Brown, Marc Tolon. *D.W. Flips!* Little, Brown, 2009.

Buehner, Caralyn, and Mark Buehner. *Snowmen at Night*.

Dial Books for Young Readers, 2018.

Carle, Eric. *From Head to Toe*. Harper Festival, an Imprint of

Harper Collins Publishers, 2018.

Carlson, Nancy L. *Loudmouth George and the Big Race*.

Lerner Publishing Group, 2004.

Chung, Arree. *Ninja!* Scholastic Inc., 2015.

Clifford, Rowan. *Rodeo Ron and His Milkshake Cows*.

Random House Children's Books UK, 2004.

Cort, Ben. *Pigs Can't Fly!* Little Tiger Press, 2003.

Craig, Lindsey, and Marc Tolon. Brown. *Dancing Feet!*

Knopf, 2012.

Cronin, Doreen, and Scott Menchin. *Stretch*. Simon &

Schuster Pub., 2009.

Cuyler, Margerly, and Hillenbrand, Will. *Please Play Safe*.

Scholastic Books, 2006.

Duchess of York, Sarah. *Helping Hands Books: Zach Gets

Some Exercise*. Sterling Children's Books, 2011.

Dunrea, Olivier. *Gemma & Gus*. Houghton Mifflin Harcourt,

2017.

Eastman, P. D. *Go, Dog, Go!* Beginner Books, 2013.

The Eentsy, Weentsy Spider Fingerplays and Action Rhymes.

Paw Prints, 2009.

Ettinger, Steve, and Pete Proctor. *Wallie Exercises*. Active

Spud Press, 2011.

Fleming, Denise. *In the Small, Small Pond*. Square Fish,

2013.

Fraser, Mary Ann. *I.Q. Gets Fit*. Walker & Co., 2007.

Fountas, Irene C. & Pinnell, Gay Su. "What is Interactive Read Aloud?" *Fountas and Pinnell Literacy Blog*, 25 January 2019, http:fpblog.fountasandpinnell.com/what-is-interactive-read-aloud.

Gogerly, Liz, et al. *Exercise*. Wayland, 2012.

Goldin, David. *Go-Go-Go!* Harry N. Abrams, 2000.

Hallinan, P.K. *Let's Be Fit*. Candy Cane Press, 2012.

Harter, Debbie. *The Animal Boogie*. Atlantic Provinces Special Education Authority, Library, 2017.

Hefele, Lynn. *Bugs and Bubbles*. Self-Published-Kindle Direct Publishing, 2013.

Hefele, Lynn. *Bugs, Flowers, and Berries*. Self-Published-Kindle Direct Publishing, 2016.

Hefele, Lynn. *Cereal Soccer*. Self-Published-Kindle Direct Publishing, 2008.

Hefele, Lynn. *Clean Up Your Backyard*. Self-Published-Kindle

Direct Publishing, 2014.

Hefele, Lynn. *Hamburger Hockey*. Self-Published-Kindle

Direct Publishing, 2015.

Hefele, Lynn. *Swish*. Self-Published-Kindle Direct Publishing,

2014.

Hefele, Lynn. *Widget's Batting Lesson*. Self-Published-Kindle

Direct Publishing, 2012.

Hefele, Lynn. *Ziny's Driving School*. Self-Published-Kindle

Direct Publishing, 2014.

Helakoski, Leslie, and Henry Cole. *Big Chickens Fly the Coop*.

Puffin Books, 2010.

Hills, Tad. *Duck & Goose*. Schwartz & Wade Books, 2017.

Jackson, Mick, and Andrea Stegmaier. *Ella May Does It Her

Way!* Words & Pictures, 2019.

Jenkins, Steve. *Biggest, Strongest, Fastest*. Houghton

Mifflin, 2009.

Jensen, Eric. *Teaching With the Brain In Mind, 2nd edition.*

ASCD, 2005.

Kang, Anna, and Christopher Weyant. *I Am (Not) Scared.*

Scholastic Singapore, 2019.

Keats, Ezra Jack. *The Snowy Day.* National Braille Press,

2019.

Kuhlman, Evan, and Chuck Groenink. *Hank's Big Day: the*

Story of a Bug. Schwartz & Wade Books, 2016.

Lambert, Jonny. *The Only Lonely Panda.* Little Tiger, 2018.

Livingston, Irene, and Brian Lies. *Finklehopper Frog.* Tricycle

Press, 2008.

London, Jonathan, and Andrew Joyner. *Duck and Hippo in*

the Rainstorm. Two Lions, 2017.

Madan CR, Singhal A. "Using actions to enhance memory:

effects of enactment, gestures, and exercise on

human memory." *Frontiers In Psychology*, vol.3, 19

Nov. 2012, doi:10.3389/fpsyg.2012.00507.

Martin, Bill, and Eric Carle. *Baby Bear, Baby Bear, What Do You See?* H. Holt, 2007.

Martin, Bill. *Barn Dance!* Macmillan, 1988.

Mayr, Diane, and Laura Rader. *Run, Turkey, Run!* Walker, 2009.

Mitton, Tony, and Guy Parker-Rees. *Down by the Cool of the Pool.* Cartwheel Books, 2017.

Murphy, Stuart J. *MathStart.* HarperCollins, 1996.

Myers, Christopher, and Yvette Lenhart. *H.O.R.S.E.: a Game of Basketball and Imagination.* Carolrhoda Books, 2015.

Noll, Sally. *Jiggle, Wiggle, Prance.* Scholastic Inc, 1993.

Olson, Jennifer Gray. *Ninja Bunny: Sister vs. Brother.* Knopf Books for Young Readers, 2016.

Pfister, Marcus. *Rainbow Fish.* North-South Books, 2019.

Pica, Rae. "Linking Literacy and Movement." *Earlychildhood NEWS, 2007,* www.earlychildhoodnews.com.

Prelutsky, Jack, and James Stevenson. *Something Big Has Been Here*. HarperCollins, 2010.

Prelutsky, Jack. *Awful Ogre's Awful Day*. HarperCollins, 2005.

Rabe, Tish. *Oh the Things You Can Do That Are Good For You*. Random House, 2001.

Raffi. *Shake My Sillies Out*. Random House International, 1999.

Ricketts, Mark. *Socco and Slurpie Cut A Rug*. Self-Published-Kindle Direct Publishing, 2016.

Ricketts, Mark. *Socco and Slurpie in P.E. Class*. Self-Published-Kindle Direct Publishing, 2017.

Ricketts, Mark. *Socco and Slurpie in the Haunted School*. Self-Published-Kindle Direct Publishing, 2015.

Ricketts, Mark. *Socco and Slurpie Join the Circus*. Self-Published-Kindle Direct Publishing, 2014.

Ricketts, Mark. *Socco and Slurpie Meet the Princess*. Self-Published-Kindle Direct Publishing, 2018.

Ricketts, Mark. *Socco and Slurpie: Beginnings*. Self-Published-Kindle Direct Publishing, 2017.

Ricketts, Mark. *Socco and Slurpie's Giant Problem- SOLVED*. Self-Published-Kindle Direct Publishing, 2017.

Ricketts, Mark. *Socco and Slurpie's Giant Problem*. Self-Published-Kindle Direct Publishing, 2105.

Ricketts, Mark. *Socco and Slurpie's Island Adventure- LOST CHAPTERS*. Self-Published-Kindle Direct Publishing, 2013.

Ricketts, Mark. *Socco and Slurpie's Island Adventure*. Self-Published-Kindle Direct Publishing, 2013.

Rockwell, Lizzy. *Busy Body Book: A Kids Guide to Fitness*. Dragonfly, 2004.

Rosen, Michael. *We're Going on a Bear Hunt*. Candlewick Press (MA), 2014.

Ryder, Joanne, and Norman Gorbaty. *Earth Dance*. Square

Fish, 2014.

Sandall, Ellie. *Follow Me!* Margaret K. McElderry Books,

2016.

Saunders, Len, and Dale Moore. *Spunky the Monkey: an*

Adventure in Exercise. Author House, 2010.

Saunders, Len, and Lauren Harvey. *Joey the Kangaroo: an*

Adventure in Exercise. Author House, 2010.

Saunders, Len. *Stretch the T. Rex: Making Fitness Fun*.

Headline Books, 2016.

Schofield-Morrison, Connie, and Frank Morrison. *I Got the*

Rhythm. Scholastic Inc., 2015.

Seuss. *The Foot Book*. HarperCollins Children's Books, 2018.

Smallman, Steve, and Neil Price. *Keep Running, Gingerbread*

Man: a Story about Keeping Active. QEB Publishing,

2015.

Smallman, Steve, and Piwowarski, Marcin. *Give Us A Smile: Cinderella*. Books and Gifts Direct, 2015.

Smallman, Steve, and Neil Price. Rapunzel, Rapunzel, Wash Your Hair!. QEB Publishing, 2015.

Smith, Charles R., and Terry Widener. *Let's Play Basketball!* Candlewick Press, 2004.

Socco and Slurpie's Island Adventure- LOST CHAPTERS. Self-Published-Kindle Direct Publishing, 2013.

Stadler, Alexander. *Beverly Billingsly Can't Catch*. Harcourt, 2004.

Stevenson, Robert Louis, and Ted Rand. *My Shadow*. Hodder & Stoughton, 1990.

Sullivan, Mary. *Ball*. Houghton Mifflin Harcourt, 2016.

Tabor, Corey R. *Fox and the Jumping Contest*. Harpercollins Publishers Inc, 2016.

Twohy, Mike. *Oops Pounce Quick Run!: an Alphabet Caper*. Scholastic Inc., 2017.

Wallace, Adam. *How to Catch the Easter Bunny*. Lake Press, 2018.

Wells, Rosemary, and Brown, Marc. *The Gulps*. Little, Brown Children, 2007.

Wegman, William. *A B C*. Hyperion, 1994.

Willan, Alex. *Jasper & Ollie*. Doubleday Books for Young Readers, 2019.

Willems, Mo. *Are You Ready to Play Outside?* Walker Books, 2013.

Willems, Mo. *Can I Play, Too?* Scholastic, Inc., 2015.

Willems, Mo. *Elephants Cannot Dance!: an Elephant & Piggie Book*. Hyperion Books for Children, 2009.

Willems, Mo. *I Love My New Toy!* Hyperion Books, 2008.

Willems, Mo. *Today I Will Fly!* Walker, 2012.

Willems, Mo. *Watch Me Throw the Ball!* Walker Books, 2013.

Williams, Linda. *The Little Old Lady Who Was Not Afraid of Anything*. Harper Collins, 1986.

Wilson, Karma, and Jane Chapman. *Bear Snores On*. McGraw-Hill Education, 2014.

Wilson, Karma, and Joan Rankin. *A Frog in the Bog*. Little Simon, 2015.

Yaccarino, Dan. *Zoom! Zoom! Zoom! I'm off to the Moon!* Scholastic, 2002.

Yolen, Jane, and Laurel Molk. *Off We Go!* Harcourt, 2003.

Yoon, Salina. *Be a Friend*. Bloomsbury, 2016.

Please check out the following picture books that I have

written. (They are available on www.amazon.com)

Socco and Slurpie's Island Adventure

Socco and Slurpie's Island Adventure: Lost Chapters

Socco and Slurpie's Giant Problem

Socco and Slurpie's Giant Problem: SOLVED

Socco and Slurpie Cut a Rug

Socco and Slurpie Meet the Princess

Socco and Slurpie Beginnings

Socco and Slurpie In P.E. Class

Socco and Slurpie Join the Circus

Socco and Slurpie in the Haunted School

Helmets, Seatbelts, and Socks: A Socco and Slurpie Safety

Story

What's In a Drink?: A Socco and Slurpie Health Story

Monster Mash-Up